THE HEALING WISDOM
OF
MARY MAGDALENE

"Thank you! This book is a welcome gift for disciples of Mary Magdalene and Jesus. Illuminating texts from the Fourth Gospel, Jack Angelo reveals the perspective of 'the woman who knew the All'—Mary Magdalene herself. Here at last, flowing from Jesus's seven miracles, are Magdalene's wisdom teachings to guide the pilgrim soul on the Way of the Heart."

MARGARET STARBIRD, AUTHOR OF *THE WOMAN WITH THE ALABASTER JAR* AND *MARY MAGDALENE, BRIDE IN EXILE*

"Jack Angelo has discovered a treasure chest to which the key has been lost for 2,000 years. In this important and fascinating book Mary Magdalene takes us into the eternal, living stream of her own consciousness and decodes for us the healing wisdom, hidden until now, in the part of the Fourth Gospel called 'The Book of Signs.' Angelo shows us how seven miracles of Jesus are intended to be a roadmap to transformation as the blessed couple both teach and model the way of total one-ness and heart-centered knowledge. Patriarchal blindness caused the message to be lost in part, but it still carries dynamic power to heal our planet and end the existential sickness that distorts much of Christian thinking. We come to realize that 'the beginning is right now' and creation is happening as we awaken to the words of Maryam, master teacher, beloved disciple, wife, and companion of Yeshua."

MARY T. BEBEN, AUTHOR OF *THE PLEIADIAN HOUSE OF INITIATION*

THE
HEALING WISDOM
OF
MARY MAGDALENE

Esoteric Secrets of the
Fourth Gospel

JACK ANGELO

Bear & Company
Rochester, Vermont • Toronto, Canada

Bear & Company
One Park Street
Rochester, Vermont 05767
www.BearandCompanyBooks.com

Bear & Company is a division of Inner Traditions International

Library of Congress Cataloging-in-Publication Data
Angelo, Jack.
  The healing wisdom of Mary Magdalene : esoteric secrets of the Fourth Gospel /
Jack Angelo.
      pages cm
  Includes bibliographical references and index.
  ISBN 978-1-59143-199-2 (pbk.) — ISBN 978-1-59143-780-2 (e-book)
  1. Mary Magdalene, Saint—Legends. 2. Mary Magdalene, Saint—Cult. 3. Bible.
John—Criticism, interpretation, etc. I. Title.
  BS2485.A596 2015
  299'.93—dc23
                                                                    2014032524

Printed and bound in the United States

10 9 8 7 6 5 4 3 2

Text design and layout by Virginia Scott Bowman
This book was typeset in Garamond Premier Pro and Clearface with Trajan Pro,
Gill Sans, and Bernhard Modern used as display typefaces

The scripture quotations contained herein are from The New Revised Standard
Version of the Bible, Anglicized Edition, copyright © 1989, 1995 by the Division
of Christian Education of the National Council of the Churches of Christ in the
United States of America, and are used by permission. All rights reserved.

To send correspondence to the author of this book, mail a first-class letter to the
author c/o Inner Traditions • Bear & Company, One Park Street, Rochester, VT
05767, and we will forward the communication, or contact the author directly at
jack@angelo5822.fsnet.co.uk.

To the memory of grandmother Anita,
Estella White, Lorna St. Aubyn,
Sir George Trevelyan.

Note to the Reader

I have kept foreign words and technical notes to a minimum. Many of them will help you set off on the adventure of discovery. My suggestions for further reading also present a set of reference points from which you can begin your own explorations.

New Testament quotations are from the Anglicized Edition of the New Revised Standard Version (NRSV) of the Bible, 1995. Old Testament quotations are inspired by the Jewish Publication Society translation of the Jewish Study Bible (JSB), 1999. Nag Hammadi Library references are from the revised edition of *The Nag Hammadi Library,* 1990.

A number of languages are used in the book. When words in a language other than English are used, they will first appear in italics. The pronunciation guide in the glossary gives an approximate version of sounds and words. Languages are fun when approached as living expressions of the human race throughout time. Just investigating a few of the words in this book will take you down some exciting paths of discovery.

CONTENTS

PART TWO

The Way Through:
Maryam's Teachings in the Gospel of Signs

PART THREE

The Seven Signs

ACKNOWLEDGMENTS

Special thanks to Jon Graham for his encouragement and belief in the book, Mindy Branstetter and all the team at Inner Traditions/Bear & Co for their dedicated approach, Jan Angelo and Gilly Adams for their support and suggestions, all those on the Red Road and Magdalene workshops. You each have a place in this book.

≈

The Sacred, the Source, and Other "Names" for God

In this book there are a number of capitalized words that indicate aspects of the Source, such as Oneness, the Holy One, the Divine, Light, the All, Godsource, Sacred Unity, as well as "soul," "spirit," and "the sacred," and "I AM." I have chosen to use androgynous, gender-inclusive God-names. But there is no name or attribute that can begin to wholly describe the infinite, all-encompassing creative force that pervades all levels of being. We reach the limits of language, where no name or attribute can contain the Infinite. They can only hint at what is essentially dynamic. This is why, when the great shaman Moses asked for its Sacred Name, the Creator's response was "ehyeh asher ehyeh," which translates not simply as "I am what I am," but simultaneously as "I will be what I will be" (Exodus 3:13–14), as Rabbi David Cooper pointed out by naming his book *God Is a Verb*. The all-encompassing creative force, I AM, is Life, a dynamic, ever-changing, process. This is what we are.

PROLOGUE

The great cave was reached after a trek through the ancient forest that covered the mountain slopes. We rounded a bend to begin the final climb up a series of stone steps that led to the walled entrance of the cave. Here, according to legend, a woman known to the world as Mary Magdalene spent the last years of her life after fleeing from Palestine. A few hundred years ago, pious Christian monks had sealed the original entrance to the cave by building a stone wall across its front, with an arched doorway flanked on either side by three stained-glass windows, to create a space like a small chapel. Outside in front was a life-size tableau of the Crucifixion complete with bleeding wounds and the distraught figure of Mary Magdalene at the foot of the Cross.

The cool, dimly lit interior contrasted with the glare of the afternoon sun outside. The walls of the cave had been left as bare rock, here and there green with moss and algae. The gloom was relieved by light coming from a few candles so that I could just make out rows of pews and darkly painted statues set into the rocky wall. The western side of the cave was shrouded in darkness, while the best-lit central area, in front of the doorway, provided a place for pilgrims to stand and take in their surroundings. I had never been here before and yet, as I stood on the threshold, there was something strangely familiar about the place, as if some distant memory was being evoked. Though the cave was furnished like a chapel, it seemed the sort of place where bats might hang from the roof in clusters and where other strange nocturnal creatures could nestle in moist crevices. Perhaps, like the caves of the Dordogne, it had been known to the Neanderthal people, but any clues to its great age were somewhat overshadowed by the stone wall and stained glass that now enclosed it.

Someone was playing a flute. I sat on a wooden pew, closed my eyes, and relaxed in the gentle atmosphere. Then, as the haunting sound of the flute began to fade, a face slowly appeared to my inner vision, the striking face of a woman with dark features and dark hair and eyes. To my surprise I felt a deep, dull ache over my heart that soon became a stabbing pain. A moment of panic. My heart was beating too fast. I was sweating. Had the exertion of climbing the mountain path been too much for me? Why now? Had I come all this way for this to happen? I rubbed my chest and tried to breathe more slowly and deeply, but instead of easing, the ache intensified. Is this what a heart attack feels like . . . could this really be my time to go? What should I do to help myself . . . and who was there in the party who would know what to do anyway? I tried to shake off these feelings, but my mind seemed gripped by thoughts of death.

I do not hear voices, as they say, but over the years I have received impressions in the silence of my mind, some of which I interpret as voice. As I struggled with my discomfort, like an answer to my anxiety, I heard the voice of a woman: "This is the pain I felt when they crucified my lord." Her voice was quiet, yet clear and strong, calm and reassuring. I was startled both by this voice and what it was saying. I had joined the party to experience the natural life of the mountain and its wild forest—the cave was to have been part of that experience.

But thoughts came rushing in. Who was this? Was it Mary Magdalene speaking, and had she been here, in this cave, for nearly two thousand years? "Are you Mary Magdalene?" I asked, suddenly aware that I was quite calmly listening to her and conversing with her. Her voice had the trace of a smile in it. "Yes," she said, "my name is Maryam."

RESTORING THE FEMININE ENERGY TO ITS RIGHTFUL PLACE

This book has been written for those who feel or sense that all is sacred and that life and the world do not have to be like they seem to be—that *we* do not have to be like we seem to be. This is a revelation of your own heart that can be felt by anyone, anywhere, no matter what path in life you may be taking. We are more than what we seem to be—to ourselves as well as to others. Life and the world are more than what they seem to be—to ourselves as well as to others.

At the time of my unsought encounter in a cave in Provence, I had been struggling with the implications posed above—where to find the "more"—and my own investigations into numerous spiritualities only brought up more questions. Following a lifelong shamanic path, I had rejected the idea that any satisfactory answers might be found within a religious context, least of all from some mythical figure of the past. However, because I was open to what some might call a "shamanic" experience, I was led to an unexpected message of discovery, coming from an entirely unexpected source: Mary Magdalene.

In a dynamic message about the profound depths of healing— available right now to all levels of life, whether individual, local, or global—her counsel to us today is that it doesn't matter whether you choose to follow the spirituality of your ancestors, your family, or your community or whether you choose a path that no one has ever taken before, as long as you follow the promptings of your heart. She says that if you really want to discover the promptings of your heart—who you are and why things are how they seem to be—you will need to embrace a new way of being that can be summed up as a heart-centered way of thinking, speaking, and acting.

The Healing Wisdom of Mary Magdalene presents Mary Magdalene's teachings on how to follow the heart-centered path: a process that she describes as crucial to human survival and to the well-being of the Earth family and our planet.

MAKING DISCOVERIES

Writers engage in research for a range of reasons, most of them linked with material for a book. Sometimes, though, they engage in research for its own sake, because it's fun to wonder where the research will lead. After my unexpected encounter with Mary Magdalene, I wondered how to share with others what had happened or whether it was something that could not, perhaps should not, be shared. At the same time I felt a profound sense of responsibility, even a compulsion, not to keep my experience with her to myself. I decided to go with these feelings and began to research this enigmatic person because I knew so little about her. The more I found out, the more fascinated I became. A startling discovery emerged—the historical person we know as Mary Magdalene was a human aspect of a great spiritual being that, existing beyond time and space, is with us today.

It is well-known that Jesus offered the world a revolutionary message of unity and equality, urging human beings to abandon the hatred and violence of the fear-based approach to life and embrace the heart-centered approach. History tells us that, to a large extent, his message has been ignored or considered impossible in practice. Less well known is the research of the last half-century revealing how Mary Magdalene and Jesus came to Earth *together* to deliver the revolutionary message and to demonstrate it through their own lives. The political process of turning Jesus into a god allowed the explosive core of their message to be overlooked, even ignored, and the role of Mary Magdalene to be erased. This book will reveal the explosive core of what continues to be a revolutionary message.

If we accept the story of Jesus the Jewish shaman-prophet, as described within mainstream Christianity, we might surmise that Mary Magdalene would have continued teaching her spiritual partner's message after his death. The evidence of discoveries made in the last century suggests that she did. Translations of formerly unknown Gnostic and Christian texts present a Mary Magdalene who was a gifted visionary teacher, best qualified to lead the Jesus movement after his death. Though these few fragments about her survive, her life as a spiritual master remains a mystery. Where, then, are the rest of her teachings? It would seem that, if they do exist, most have either been skillfully sabotaged or carefully kept secret. *The Healing Wisdom of Mary Magdalene* addresses the reasons for the former and the exciting evidence for the latter.

I believe that I have discovered a coherent body of her teachings hidden in one of the canonical gospels and that these are directly linked to the message that she and Jesus proclaimed. One of the many surprises about her teachings is their timeless quality, making them even more relevant to us today than they might have been to the people of two thousand years ago. In this book the healing wisdom of her teachings about the heart-centered approach to life is presented for the first time.

There is scholarly opinion that Mary Magdalene was the author of the Fourth Gospel, not a person named John. My own research indicates that the Fourth Gospel has both housed and protected some of her teachings. The sequence of events that led to the creation of the initially unnamed Fourth Gospel may well have gone as follows. In common with Semitic teachers of the time, Mary Magdalene taught orally, using a dramatic story form to encode her spiritual lessons. As a reaction to the pressures of the times, and in order to preserve her teachings, the decision was made to write them down. When members of the movement, such as Peter and Andrew, broke away from Mary Magdalene's leadership, they took with them a copy of the written version of her teachings. These were later edited and redacted to form a gospel that conformed to the dogma of the new Christian religion. This gospel presents a series of episodes in the life of Jesus as a background to his radical spiritual message.

THE GOSPEL OF SIGNS

However, even in its current gospel form, Mary Magdalene's teachings will be revealed to anyone who is prepared to live with the text, absorb its atmosphere, and feel its gentle wisdom. Scholars have named the first eleven chapters of the Fourth Gospel the "Gospel of Signs" because the text describes seven miracles of Jesus as "signs." Using a time-honored method of holistic, intuitive investigation, I discovered that the episodic stories in the Gospel of Signs are deliberately multilayered and that their apparent simplicity conceals a startling secret: the seven miracles are in fact signs pointing to seven key steps to personal transformation and healing.

The levels of meaning within Mary Magdalene's Teaching Story would have proved an exhilarating inspiration to members of her community, helping them to experience the energetic presence of the shaman-prophet Jesus in their journey of transformation. For example, the Story describes the shamanic healing of a blind person when Jesus spits on clay dirt and smears the paste over the blind man's eyes. The deeper meaning of this "sign" is about perceiving with the "eyes of the heart" to become aware of the profound connection between our individual healing and the healing of the world. Chapter 15, "Sign Six" fleshes out and celebrates this pivotal episode.

MASCULINE AND FEMININE

We are living in a period of rapid change. Many people are creating new forms of spirituality that feel comfortable and resonate for them. It is no coincidence that women are in the vanguard of this evolutionary movement. Since my encounter with Mary Magdalene in 1988, I have been running Earth-based retreats and workshops in healing and personal transformation. In every one of them, women outnumbered the men by at least two to one. It seemed to me that women, far more than men, were responding to the growing feminine force bringing about changes in energy and consciousness, especially through feminine expressions of spirituality, ritual, and ceremony. There is also evidence that men are being stirred by the feminine force and are awakening to it.

All subtle energy healers know that human beings, regardless of gender, operate with two essential energy streams, known as the "feminine" and the "masculine." From an energetic point of view, human life has been out of balance for a few thousand years through the domination of a patriarchal masculine energy. The evidence suggests that, if unchecked, the ongoing manifestation of the masculine will accelerate the destruction of lives, whole communities and natural environments, and the rate of exploitation of finite resources, leading to disaster for all on planet Earth.

Mary Magdalene teaches that the state of imbalance is *our* problem; thus the healing of our relationship with the Earth and Nature depends on healing our relationship with ourselves and each other. To begin the healing process, the feminine energy has to be restored to its rightful place and brought into balance with the masculine. This is a process that has, in fact, been slowly taking place for centuries as women in different societies and cultures have fought for recognition, emancipation, and equality. Today, the growing surge in the feminine energy force is far more evident worldwide with the struggle to make balance and harmony a reality. Along with these struggles, human beings are also becoming aware of, and seeking to communicate with, spiritual manifestations of the feminine to help bring about the necessary energetic changes. As a powerful embodiment of the feminine force, the spiritual teacher we call Mary Magdalene is continuing to penetrate human consciousness and signs of her spiritual presence are already challenging the imbalances that have been perpetuated and accepted in every society.

The Healing Wisdom of Mary Magdalene has been a pilgrimage for me as well as a voyage of discovery. The book will take you on a similar journey. In Part One I describe a literary version of an archaeological dig as I set about my search for Mary Magdalene, the teacher and mystic. The search took me through a fascinating labyrinth of sacred texts to provide a rich portrayal that contrasted with the strangely limited portrait of her in the Christian New Testament.

Part Two prepares you for the core of the transformative sacred journey through the Seven Signs. In Part Three you will explore the Signs starting with a current biblical text and reaching the profound revelations that each Sign holds. I use the term "transformative" with a proviso: the teachings have to be *practiced*. Mary Magdalene warns that simply reading about them will not bring about changes in your consciousness or your life: regular practice will.

ACHIEVING TWENTY-FIRST-CENTURY CONSCIOUSNESS

The people of the world are realizing, at last, that great spiritual masters come here for all of us. No religion, race, or culture owns them. For important soul reasons, each one of them chooses to be born into a certain place and at a certain time. Thus, their lives and teachings reflect the times and places in which they lived as physical beings. But this should not blind us to the reality that their teachings belong to all of us, not to a specific religious group, race, or culture. True spiritual masters may be recognized as those whose teachings resonate with all times and all places.

Mary Magdalene is one such spiritual master. However, it is essential not to focus on the historical person who lived in the Middle East two millennia ago. You will not get any closer to your sacred self by agonizing about who she was, whether she was married or bore children, and where she ended up, for she transcends personhood. This being is better thought of as a powerful, loving, spiritual force that can be called upon in our time to help us solve the problems caused by our sense of separation from each other, and our disconnection from the sacred.

It is a joyful fact that mysteries hidden for nearly two thousand years still have the power to speak to all human beings and address the state of the world today. The voice is loud and clear. *The Healing Wisdom of Mary Magdalene* unlocks the hidden mysteries of Mary Magdalene's Teaching Story to gift us all—irrespective of religion, spiritual outlook, ethnicity, gender, or sexuality—with the guidance and healing wisdom to achieve the consciousness that arises in the heart alone.

Mary Magdalene has been aware of this book from the time I first began to dream about it many years ago. In the final chapter she updates the teachings revealed by each Sign, giving further power to their contemporary relevance.

This is what I am going to share with you.

PART ONE

*Discovering
Mary Magdalene
the Teacher*

1

A CHILDHOOD VISION

Bristol 1941. Bombs are falling on the countryside where we live. Luftwaffe planes are attacking the city, raining down incendiary devices and high explosives. They are aiming for the docks, the railways, and the aircraft factories. We have lost our house and everything in it. The world is at war. I later learn that "the Good Friday raids" killed a thousand people and injured thousands more.

The wail of a siren still takes me back to being carried in my mother's arms to a garden shelter. I can feel my mother's panic, smell her sweat, hear her panting for breath. My nostrils are clogged with dust and the smell of destruction. I look up into the dark indigo sky and see the searchlights, like giant fingers of light, pointing out the dark shapes of the bombers with their deadly cargo, and stars in their hundreds. I hear the dreadful hum of engines overhead and the boom-boom of anti-aircraft guns below them. The air crackles with the sound of explosions and breaking glass, with distant shouts and screams. There is panic and despair. Why isn't my dad here to help us?

On such a night I have a dream. The scene is a sandy beach with palm trees at either end, gently sloping down to the calm blue waters of the sea. The sun shines in a clear blue sky. At the water's edge is a long line of men, women, and children, all holding hands and looking out to sea. They are completely naked and their light brown skin glows in the sunlight. I awake with a profound feeling of delight, though I have never seen a beach, a palm tree, or the sea, and I have never seen a brown person, let alone a naked one. I am two years old.

We all have dreams. Sometimes our dreams are in vivid color and they remain with us for a lifetime. These visionary dreams are given to us as memorable communications directly from the soul. We may get the message immediately, but it can also take many years for us to discover what we have been shown.

Like most infants, when I was two I was more soul-child than Earth-child, still in touch with the sacred aspect of my being. But there was hardship, suffering, and anxiety as the world around me was disintegrating. In contrast the beach vision was showing me a quite different world. In it people are together in harmony—the Earth and sea are at peace. There is an atmosphere of warmth, color, serenity, safety, and love. There is joy in union with one another and with the environment. I was taken to a place within myself where this reality was always affirmed, a place of love and light in the middle of my chest that I now call the "Heart Space." This was my safe place to retreat to.

Like a soothing balm to the painful reality of life at the time, the beach vision showed me that the world in conflict should not be like that. Life should be like the beach scene, which I had sensed as a beautiful feeling. Over the years I came to understand that the "beautiful feeling" was about the deep harmony of oneness. I have found myself measuring life experience against that sense of oneness, that beautiful feeling, that childhood vision of the beach.

2

THE VOICE
IN THE CAVE

I bless my mother for introducing me, at a very young age, to books.
The best of them could be read aloud and often began with the words
"once upon a time." This magical phrase promised an intriguing tale
with strong characters and enough surreal elements to arouse my curiosity. They also promised a satisfying conclusion with the words "and
they all lived happily ever after," a simple formula that allowed the characters to go on living in my imagination in a future filled with cheer-
ful expectation. Stories describe and illuminate our lives; some have the
power to draw us in so that we feel like characters in the story itself.

A CAVE ENCOUNTER IN
THE SOUTH OF FRANCE

Once upon a time I was earning a precarious living as a writer and seeking inspiration. In the spring of 1988, I was sitting in a café at my usual
table by the communal notice board. As my coffee cooled, I glanced up
to survey what had been posted. Among the ads for Hopi ear candle
therapy and a washing machine going cheap, a small blue sheet caught
my eye, announcing an "Essene Seminar with Sir George Trevelyan."
It proposed two weeks at a "delightful Center in Provence." I calcu-
lated that I could just about afford the cost, along with the airfare to

Marseille. I knew very little about the Essenes or Sir George Trevelyan, but as I reread the list of subjects that would be covered during the two weeks, into my mind came my beach vision. I could not fathom why this should be so and dismissed the image; after all it wasn't advertised as a beach holiday with nude beach frolics. I told myself that I deserved an intriguing, and possibly relaxing, holiday in the South of France, and it could be just the inspiration that the writer in me so desperately needed.

With the mountains of the Luberon to the south, the study center nestled on a hillside of orange soil terraced with olive and almond trees. The theme of the seminar was a view of Essene spirituality with its grounding in Nature and the seasons; but this theme soon expanded to range from the Cathars and Bogomils to the poetry of Wordsworth. Then came the announcement that there was to be a trip to the ancient mountain cave of Sainte Baume. Most of us agreed that this would be a welcome change from indoor lectures.

The day before the trip, I came across a little guide book saying that, once a place for pilgrimage to ancient fertility goddesses, a Christian tradition has it that after fleeing from Palestine, Mary Magdalene found sanctuary in the Sainte Baume cave where she spent the last years of her life meditating and teaching. To present a balanced view, or perhaps as a deterrent to the gullible, the text continued: "However, various authorities have questioned whether the Magdalene ever came to Gaul, and, if she did, whether she would have chosen such a huge and draughty cave in which to settle." With both these views in mind, I looked forward with expectation to the following day.

During our trek through the forest to reach our destination, Sir George enthused about the cave and the good memories it held for him. He recalled how, on a previous visit, he had "seen" an image of Pan. This was a delightful surprise, for he was very fond of Pan as a nature divinity and always wondered if he would see him again at Sainte Baume. These remarks created excitement in the group, and we began to wonder what experiences we might have.

We rounded a bend to begin the final climb up a series of stone steps that led to the cave. A few hundred years ago, Dominican monks built a stone wall across the original entrance, with an arched doorway flanked on either side by three stained-glass windows, creating a small chapel. In front was a life-size, vivid tableau of the Crucifixion including the distraught figure of Mary Magdalene at the foot of the Cross.

The interior was dim and cool, a contrast to the bright outdoors. The cave had the furnishings of a chapel, but with an earthy feeling as well, alive with nature. In the light of a few candles, I stood on the threshold. I had never been there, yet the place seemed to evoke a deep memory.

I sat on a wooden pew, closed my eyes, and waited. I was looking forward to a possible sighting of Pan, the ancient guardian-spirit of Nature. Suddenly I heard the haunting sound of a flute. The pipes of Pan! I couldn't resist opening an eye. There, in front of the altar stood a Japanese tourist playing a *shakuhachi* flute. Chuckling at my skepticism, I closed my eyes and the next moment was startled to see a smiling greenish-brown face that shone with a golden light. So Pan really did appear in this cave. "Are you Pan?" I asked, mentally. Instead of an answer, the face continued to grin at me for a few more moments and then began to fade.

I rested in the haunting sound of the flute. But as I was musing on this, the face of Pan was replaced by the face of a young woman with dark features and dark hair and eyes. Then came a dull ache in my chest that quickly transformed to a stabbing pain. Panic flooded me. "Jack collapsed and died in the Grotto of Sainte Baume. He had lived in France but had never visited Provence before," I imagined the obituary to read. I was gripped with fear and thoughts of death.

As I struggled with these sensations, I heard her voice: "This is the pain I felt when they crucified my lord." Immediately, my mind was awash with questions. Who was this? Was it Mary Magdalene speaking, and had she been there for nearly 2,000 years? "Are you Mary Magdalene?" I asked, aware that I was calmly listening to her and conversing with her. I could hear the smile in her voice. "Yes," she said, "my name is Maryam." I found out later that Maryam was her original Aramaic name and that in the Semitic culture of the time, "my lord" was the normal way of describing a husband, in fact, the modern Hebrew word for husband, *ba'al,* also translates as "lord."

MARYAM'S MESSAGE

When contact is made with a spirit being, the mind is often confused, desperately trying to make sense of what is happening. I wanted to keep calm and yet remain open. Meanwhile, a more parental voice was urging me to remember where I was and at all costs be polite. So containing my excitement, I found myself asking: "Is there anything you wish to tell me?" Straight away she said,

You are all Christs, or Christs in the making. It is only your clouded vision that prevents you from seeing that you are all beings of light. It does not matter if no one believes what you say, but I want you to tell the others that Jesus, the Master, is walking among you right now. . . . The pain you feel is my pain. I cannot let you feel all of the pain because you could not bear it. It is my signal to you that it is Mary Magdalene whom you sense. . . . You can call on me any time to help you and I will use this signal to assure you that I am close. It cannot hurt you, it is just my signal.

She then gave me her blessing.

I sensed that Maryam knew how the word "Christ" jarred with me as a non-Christian. But at the same moment, I realized that, for her, names and titles did not matter and my challenge was not to focus on them. She had carefully chosen the word favored by the church. I knew that in Greek a *khristos* was an "anointed one." Maryam was telling me that we are all born anointed—with an inner messiah—while most of us are immersed in the process of awakening to this fact. So the title was not exclusive to Jesus . . . even though he was walking among us. Then what was the significance of being anointed, I wondered. I would carry out her request, though it might prove difficult or even offensive to some of the group.

I had the feeling that time was running out, that this "conversation" might end as quickly as it had begun. What an opportunity! Reeling with the thought that I was "talking" to Mary Magdalene, my mind flooded with questions. Which were the most important? What did I need to know? So the most banal question came out first: "Is the story about you and Joseph of Arimathea coming to France and living in this cave true?" Her voice seemed to smile again, calming me and slowing me down. She would not be drawn. She continued,

◆ ————————————————————————————

I am here. I can be wherever people need me to be. It does not matter whether the story is true or not. Look behind the words. See the force behind the story. You can call on me any time to help you and I will use this signal to assure you that I am close. It cannot hurt you. It is my signal to you that it is I, Mary Magdalene, whom you sense . . . I am going now . . . It is time for you to go too.

I became conscious of the group members shifting about, moving off. Her voice was still there, reassuring me: "Call upon me when you wish. You know what my signal will be." And then . . . nothing, only space where she used to be. It was too soon for me to go. I sat in the pew feeling stunned. Maryam was there, speaking to me. Why me? I needed time to readjust. Pain would be her signal. Was that like the pain I had felt as a small child when the world around me was being destroyed? She was feeling the pain of the world then, and she is still feeling the pain of the world now. My thoughts were interrupted by a hand on my shoulder. The group was leaving. Near the door to the outside, there was a stone bowl set into the wall, filled with sanctified water

into which pilgrims could dip their fingers and bless themselves. I saw
it for the first time as if it had been put there to aid my exit. It struck
me that I had been in another kind of womb and that I was emerging
once again into the light. I looked again at the bizarre iconography of
torture and death: the passionate figure of Mary Magdalene and the
bleeding Jesus. Immediately, my own forceps birth, via my mother's
blood-smeared legs, confronted me: I could smell the scent of blood and
pain. The next day was Good Friday.

Later that evening the group assembled and we were invited to
share our experiences of the trip to Sainte Baume. My cave experience
was received with polite silence. Back in my room I wrote up the day in
my journal. On rereading the account I was gripped by an overwhelm-
ing sense that Maryam was asking me to do something, but I had no
idea what that something might be.

I never heard from any of the group whether my account had any
effect on them or not. The rest of the seminar passed very quickly. I
was aware of lectures, aware of George Trevelyan's sonorous voice as he
recited poetry by Wordsworth and Thomas Traherne, and again when
he read the Essene meditations for the day. But behind George's voice
was the voice of Maryam, and behind his carefully chosen words, her
words became lines of poetry, the music of the evening circle dances and
the song of the cicadas.

The flight from Marseille back to the UK was delayed for an hour.
I sat in the waiting area and gazed around at the airport surroundings,
the groups of people on their way to different destinations. I listened to
the announcements delivered in French and English. It all seemed a very
different world from where I had recently been staying. Who here would
want to know about Mary Magdalene, La Madeleine, let alone believe
that she talked to pilgrims in a Provençal cave? I glanced up at the moving
announcement board. It now displayed the phrase: "What do you need to
know?" In my mind I told myself: I need to know about you, Maryam. I
know virtually nothing. I'm going to find out who you are, why you gave
me that message, and what—if anything—your message means.

3

LOOKING BEHIND
THE WORDS

When we look back at some of the problems that have come our way, especially those which cause distress and anxiety, we can see how they often lead us onto a new path in life.

DISCOVERING DISTANT HEALING

Three years before my encounter with Mary Magdalene, I was suffering with severe back trouble and my editor had put me in touch with a well-known healer, Dennis Barrett, who happened to live in Bristol. As I made my way to his home, a memory flooded back of greeting my father off the train on his return from the war and being lifted up into his arms.

After a few sessions Dennis encouraged me to investigate the world of hands-on healing and to take up healing myself. He gave no clue as to how to get started as a healer, assuring me that it would happen when the time was right. His only piece of advice was: "If you don't like people, don't bother to try healing."

Soon after that, on a writing trip to Italy, I stayed in a large family home. The house was quiet as I lay awake planning my research. Suddenly a rasping sound broke the silence. Grandfather was coughing. On and on he coughed until the coughs changed to groans and cries of desperation. The rest of the house remained still. No one went to his aid. Perhaps the family slept through it because they were already used to these harrowing sounds and they felt powerless to bring him any form of relief. I wanted to help him and felt impressed to hold my hands out in his direction to send some healing. To my surprise my palms and fingertips began tingling as I mentally asked for help to be sent to the old man. The next moment his coughing stopped abruptly. The house returned to silence and I dropped off to sleep.

In the small hours of the next night, the old man began to cough again, hardly able to pause for breath. I stretched out my hands and asked for help to come to him, and again his coughing stopped. As the week went on, the grandfather's coughing began to ease, and on my last night it, had almost disappeared. This was my first venture into distant healing. Unlike traditional hands-on healing where the healer is present with the subject, in distant healing the healer sends out healing energy, or a prayer for healing, to the subject who is at some distance from the healer. The great advantage of this form of healing is that the subject can be a person, an animal, a plant, an environment, or even a situation, and they can be at any distance.

On my return to Wales, I had plenty of opportunities to practice distant healing and to see if it actually produced positive results. On many occasions results extended beyond healing people of conditions to changing situations for the better. I kept a working journal and built up a useful database of practice that gave me an excellent grounding and understanding when I began to work "hands-on." Two years later I was in the cave at Sainte Baume.

At school I had dreams of becoming an artist, but my parents wanted me to study science. On leaving school I had no idea what to do with my qualifications. I spent a few years learning how to farm before becoming a teacher. Much later my encounter with Mary Magdalene was a turning point: from then on I felt driven to study subtle energy medicine and hands-on healing. However, I could see little hope of earning a living from either healing practice or its studies.

Out of the blue my editor called to say that the publishing house wanted someone to write the biography of Dennis Barrett the healer, and that my experiences and friendship with him made me the ideal candidate for the project. During a series of interviews, I asked Dennis how healing worked. "With love," he said. "It comes from the source of love, goes through me and into the patient. It's love that does the healing." This definition may sound naive, but at the time it sounded reasonable to me that love could heal, and after years of research and experience, I find that Dennis's definition still holds true. Just as Dennis described them, my experience is that healing energies come from the Source of energy—the Oneness that some people call God. Dennis was delighted with his story *The Healing Spirit*. People continue to borrow the book from their local library twenty years later, and I still hear from readers all over the world.

YOUR HEALING POWER

Now that I was writing about healing, including my own experience, it seemed time to look at how the healing power of love actually worked. I began to look more deeply into the mechanics and meaning of healing. My years at school studying the sciences trained me to be skeptical and to look at outcomes and the reason for them. I saw that there were plenty of books about different aspects of healing: subtle energies (those that travel faster than the speed of light), energy fields, subtle energy centers (chakras), the power of intention, the origin of healing energies, and so on, but all this information was not available under one cover. I decided to combine the different facets of healing with my own experience to create one book, as a handbook for healers and anyone interested in the subject. This book was *Your Healing Power*. It has since become an international healing classic, published in the United States as *Hands-On Healing*.

Your Healing Power is addressed to as wide an audience as possible, avoiding claims that because it is a spiritual discipline, it is linked to a particular religion. It is salutary to recall that whoever we are, the spirituality of our distant ancestors was shamanic and that shamanism is the basis of all spiritual streams. The shaman, of either gender, is able to demonstrate to the group or tribe a genuine connection with—and a profound understanding of—the sacred, the source of healing, and the source of healing energies. Archaeological evidence suggests that this has been so during at least the 100,000 years of human history.

THE SHAMANIC WORLDVIEW

As I listened to people presenting their conditions, I began to realize that each condition was also about a relationship—with themselves as well as with others—a situation, or an environment and that the healing needed to go beyond the person. These conclusions came together when I started looking at the way indigenous people interacted with each other, their holistic attitudes toward sickness, and how ritual and ceremony played a vital part in the everyday life of the people. Here, the emotional, mental, and spiritual, as well as the physical health of individuals, was intimately entwined with the health of the group, and vice versa. This reflects the shamanic worldview that we are all one—with each other, with the world around us, with the cosmos, and with the realm of spirit.

I came across a living shamanic worldview when I made contact with Native Americans of the Lakota nation. With their respect for the sacred nature of all beings I felt that I had come home. The Lakota affirmation used before and after any sacred ceremony, *mitakuye oyasin,* "we are all related," is the same declaration of Oneness that was graphically represented in my beach vision. My passionate interest in shamanism and the natural world soon led me to work with the healing ways of many indigenous peoples, especially Native Americans. Even though I was only able to work with these "medicine" people for a few days at a time, I found that they were able to transmit further teachings at a distance. Sometimes I would wake up knowing that I had just received a teaching during my sleep.

I did not realize at the time that I was formulating a language with which I could share such experiences: a language that could describe our interconnectedness and interdependence with each other and with the whole environment, while at the same time being aware of these events as energetic transactions. Through my experiences in subtle energy medicine and shamanic healing, I absorbed a way of looking at these things, finding a language that later proved an invaluable preparation for the work of unraveling the mysteries of Maryam's teaching stories. She talks about the four worlds of the human being—the physical, emotional, mental, and the spiritual—and the life journey, using the language of healing, of love, and the shamanic worldview.

MY INVESTIGATION BEGINS

While Mary Magdalene was speaking to me during the Easter of 1988, the world continued to be at war as the energies of conflict expanded into Afghanistan, a country that in the 1960s and 1970s, had been so hospitable to people from anywhere. With my beach vision I had been shown that life should not be in conflict like this. There had to be an explanation for the contrast between my internal vision and the recurring external reality. There had to be an answer and I guessed that it would have to be some form of healing, some form of love.

As my writing career was taking a turn for the better, behind all the bustle of work and teaching commitments, I continued to feel the strong presence of Mary Magdalene. I was still asking myself why an excursion to meet the nature spirit Pan had morphed into an encounter with Maryam. Her words had been dazzling, brief, and to the point. Her remark "You are all Christs, or Christs in the making . . . only your clouded vision prevents you from seeing that you are beings of light," continued to resound in my mind. What clouds our vision?

I strived to answer this question, and the more pressing question of "why." Along with my work as a writer and teacher in the field of subtle energy medicine, I began to study every text I could find to satisfy a burning curiosity about who Maryam was and what had happened to her.

Anyone who sets out on such a quest soon makes the disquieting discovery that the early Christian church had a paranoid fear of anything other than its own version of the personhood of Jesus and the purpose of his short earthly life. This fear continues among the diverse expressions of Christianity today. In the religion's infancy a new word entered the language: "heresy," from the Greek *airesis* meaning "having a choice," so that anyone choosing to have a view that differed from Christian dogma was branded a heretic. This classification was extended to people of other religions, including Judaism, leading to centuries of horrendous torture, execution, and murder of those who chose to disagree: a picture that made me both angry and disappointed. I would investigate the heretical as well as the canonical material, bearing in mind that what someone wants to hide from you is often what you need to look at first.

During his life as a spiritual teacher, the early followers of Jesus, like other Jewish spiritual groups, described themselves as "people of the Way." The Way was the revolutionary way of life taught by spiritual masters like Jesus. The word Christ was a later title given to Jesus, derived from the Greek khristos (meaning "anointed one"). Even the name Jesus comes to us via the Greek Yesous. Author and theologian Jean-Yves Leloup honors the Middle Eastern origins of Jesus by using his Hebrew name Yeshua, a name that implies the saving grace of the Godsource. Throughout the rest of this book, I shall do the same. For over two hundred years after his execution, numerous accounts of his life and teachings were compiled by different groups within the Yeshua movement, each with their own needs and agendas. However, the movement existed within a strongly patriarchal culture that was reluctant to give equality to women. Though there was a liberal and open approach to spiritual practice throughout the Middle East, it seems that the presence of women in the movement began to cause problems for many male followers.

GNOSTIC HERESY

In contrast to the Christian insistence on salvation through faith in the deified Jesus, I learned that long before he was born, the ancient mystery schools of the Middle East and Greece were teaching that the most valuable spiritual experience was *gnosis,* or knowledge. But this gnosis had nothing to do with following dogma to the letter and everything to do with the actual, or inner, knowing that takes place within the heart. Thus "gnostic" became the generic Greek word for one who sought direct experience of the Source. Around the time of Yeshua the followers of a form of revolutionary Galilean Judaism (and later Christianity) based on the principal of gnosis came to be called "Gnostics." For the petrified patriarchs of the early church, however, Gnostic became synonymous with heretical so that all writings considered to be Gnostic were vilified and, wherever possible, destroyed: a policy that automatically applied to Gnostic believers too.

FINDING MARYAM IN
THE NAG HAMMADI LIBRARY

This policy obviously encouraged more open-minded spiritual seekers to be very careful and, if necessary, to hide their sacred texts where they could not easily be found, in the hope that they could be retrieved when more liberal times returned. Around 450 CE the occupants of a small Coptic monastery near the northern Egyptian town of Nag Hammadi did just that, sealing a whole library of Gnostic and other texts in an earthenware jar and burying it deep in the sand at the foot of a rocky cliff. Better times did not return, and the story of its discovery in 1945 by peasant farmers is both banal and dramatic.

The farmers were on their way to a revenge killing when they stopped to dig for fertilizer and unearthed the jar. It was said that as one of them broke open the jar, a cloud of golden dust rose into the air. Back at their home, finding that the leather-bound texts were written in languages that she could not fathom, the mother began to tear out pages to get a cooking fire going. However, the canny farmers realized that they might get a good price for the cache and took the rest to market. What was left of the precious texts eventually found their way into the hands of academics and translators who, fearing the wrath of the church, kept their findings under wraps for thirty years.

However, the truth came out and translations began to appear in the 1970s. The fabled golden cloud seems to me a metaphor for the light that has since been shed on the diverse reality of early Christianity and Gnosticism, helping to link those religious streams with their ancestry in the mystery traditions of the ancient Middle East. Maybe even people today need to discover these links. Their contents, however, would have created problems for the church.

Many of the so-called Gnostic texts, including the Gospel of Thomas, the Gospel of Philip, and the Dialogue of the Savior, present a great deal of information about Maryam, explaining how she was greatly loved by Yeshua and providing evidence to show that she was the disciple most qualified to carry on the leadership of the movement. The Gospel of Philip says that Yeshua was always kissing Maryam, and describes her with the Greek word *koinonos*. This word implies an intimate coupling, meaning that she was a close spiritual, perhaps sexual, companion to Yeshua (63.30–64.9). According to the Gospel of Philip, the existential sickness of humanity results from the failure to see and experience the feminine and masculine energy streams, and so the two sexes, as a unity. However, the demonstration of this unity, in the loving relationship between Yeshua and Maryam, was stirring up jealousy and unrest among some of the male disciples.

THE GOSPEL OF MARY

There is further evidence of this schism in the Gospel of Mary (Magdalene). Though this manuscript was not part of the Nag Hammadi cache, its language sounds and feels so much like the three scriptures named above that it is surprising it was not found among these texts. First discovered in 1896 in a Cairo market by a German collector of antiquities, an English translation did not appear until the 1970s. Like the Nag Hammadi texts, the Gospel of Mary appears to be a fourth- or fifth-century Coptic copy of an earlier second-century scripture. It presents clear evidence of Maryam as teacher as well as follower, featuring her visionary powers and ability to receive teachings about the soul from Yeshua.

The scripture tells how a small group of disciples (Peter, Andrew, Levi) ask her to describe some of these teachings. In a vision Yeshua first explains to Maryam that it is quite natural for humans to be able to receive visions or other forms of communication from spirit. He is about to give her a teaching but, tantalizingly, the next few pages of her account have been torn from the text. Why and by whom? I wondered. However, what still remains appears to be a teaching about the soul's journey here in the physical world and how a person can learn to break out of the bondage of ignorance, of not being conscious of their divine reality. The text indicates that, via the vision, Maryam was able to see the world as it really is and thus find deep inner peace from such knowledge.

This was as exciting for me to read as it was shocking for the male disciples to hear from Maryam's lips. We are left with the male disciples angry and bewildered. They had never come across such teachings, and anyway why, they asked, should they change their customs to accept what a woman says? But what really presses Peter's buttons is his assumption that Yeshua thought more of Maryam than he did of the men. Maryam is shocked by his violent outburst and, weeping, asks how he could think that she would lie about what Yeshua had conveyed to her in teachings that were for all of them. It is left to Levi (curiously, his name contains the Hebrew word *lev,* or heart) to admonish the men for sounding like their misogynistic enemies; they should avoid their negative attitudes and instead try to become balanced human beings and use their energy to spread the good news about how to achieve that state. It is Levi who tells us that Peter had always been hot-tempered and that Yeshua had a special love for Maryam. This final scene, when added to the evidence in the Gospel of Philip, clearly illustrates why most of the male disciples, led by Peter and Andrew, disdained her leadership and went their own way to found the patriarchal Christian church. History shows us that in doing so, they completely missed the point about who the two human beings Yeshua and Maryam were and the wisdom path of love that they exemplified as well as proclaimed.

REVEALING THE REVEALER

I mention only some of the surprises to be found in the Nag Hammadi Library, but perhaps the most exciting surprise for me was the book that, somewhat like the Gospel of Mary, showed why Maryam was so obviously the teacher and leader of the Yeshua movement after the Crucifixion. This text is the Dialogue of the Savior, a second-century compilation of an ancient Gnostic work began in the first century when the Fourth (John) Gospel was being compiled. The Dialogue also follows the Semitic theme of a dialogue with the teacher, where the advanced disciples are Judas, Thomas, Matthew, and Maryam. The text is considered to be close to the language of the Fourth Gospel in that it gives an interpretation of the sayings of Yeshua in the light of the group's experience of gnosis (inner knowing).

Here, many of the rich mystical teachings of Yeshua hint at the profound depths of the Gospel of Mary and those I was to find later in the Fourth Gospel. Equally amazing is the way the text also honors Maryam as "the woman who knew the All," meaning that, like Yeshua, she had complete spiritual realization. The Dialogue of the Savior describes her as the "apostle who excels the rest," superior to both Thomas and Matthew, who also had inner teachings from Yeshua. She completely understood his teachings and taught others about them (139:12–13). In her eagerness to grasp the meaning of life, she declares: "I want to understand all things, just as they are." Those who will achieve this understanding, counsels Yeshua, will seek out life because the divine is in life, not somewhere else. This is exactly what life has to offer: an encounter with the divine, and this is the only true wealth, says Yeshua (140:69).

Earlier, when she asks Yeshua why she had come to planet Earth, he tells her: "You make clear the abundance of the revealer" (140:14–18). These conversations, radiating wisdom and shining like beacons of hope, clearly define Maryam's cosmic mission—she came to bring clarity about the Source and reveal the immanent presence of the Divine.

MARYAM: A HUMAN EMBODIMENT OF THE SACRED FEMININE

With the discovery and translation of the Nag Hammadi Library, Maryam dances from the pages of history once again. Like her female prophet namesake, Miriam, she chants and plays the tambourine to summon up vital spiritual energies. When she asks Yeshua questions, she is confronting the masculine view. When she is teaching she is giving the feminine view. When she is dialoging she is expressing the feminine voice. It was natural that the male disciples would find it difficult to accept the feminine perspective because it just did not happen in their culture. The feminine has a totally different way of expressing, reacting, responding, teaching, exploring, and so on. Finally, the historical records clearly demonstrate that Maryam was the human embodiment of the sacred feminine and not just a woman called Mary Magdalene.

Her leadership may have been disdained by the breakaway group, but they seemed to have overlooked even the words of the male figure they revered. Maryam's qualifications to lead the Jesus movement and teach its followers were actually well known. Now I was really getting somewhere. The one other text I wanted to consult had been found much earlier in Egypt, but had nothing to do with the Nag Hammadi Library. Even if it painted a completely different portrait of Maryam, I wanted to know about it.

THE MARYAM OF THE PISTIS SOPHIA

In the face of persecution, a holy book would also be cunningly hidden where it would not look out of place among other innocuous leather-bound texts. Perhaps this was how, in 1773, a century before the discovery of the Gospel of Mary, during his travels in Egypt, a Dr. Askew acquired a bundle of Gnostic material that he later sold to the British Museum as an Egyptian curiosity. These are late second-century CE texts written in Coptic. Certain scholars soon realized the implications of publishing these texts and made sure that they did not reach the public domain in English until the early 1900s. Amid the translated bundle was a book called Pistis Sophia ("Faith of Wisdom"), a title that juxtaposes two Greek words. *Pistis* is not blind faith, but rather an inner knowing, like gnosis, and *sofia* is not knowledge gained by experience but intuitive knowledge as an aspect of divine love. According to the blurb on the back cover of the translation, it contained previously unknown and controversial material about both Jesus and Mary Magdalene. If this was so, there was a good chance that it would confirm the amazing revelations I had discovered in the books of the Nag Hammadi Library.

In both Hebrew and Greek, "wisdom" is a feminine word (Hb. *khokhmah,* Gr. *sofia*). The Jewish sacred book known as Proverbs features a feminine being called Wisdom. Since the Pistis Sophia is about how the journey of embodied Wisdom relates to us as human travelers, I turned down the byway of Proverbs to see what she had to say. The book is described as the wise words of King Solomon, but I was intrigued by the way the text moves into and out of the voice of Wisdom as a feminine entity who speaks in the simple and direct language of the heart. She explains that as an aspect of the Source, she existed long before the Creation and witnessed its genesis (8:22–31). If we are awake and aware, we will find that she calls to us from every facet of life. Her way is pleasant and all her paths are peace, we are told, and she is literally a Tree of Life to those who embrace her (3:17–18). I was fascinated now to see if there would be a connection between the feminine energy known as Wisdom and the Mary Magdalene portrayed in the Faith of Wisdom story.

In a graphic way of illustrating how the soul moves from the vibrations of the spirit world to the relative density of the physical universe, the Pistis Sophia presents a description of how Sophia/Wisdom "descends" into the life of the universe and how Jesus the Christ awakens her faith in her spiritual reality to guide her back to her home in the Source. The story takes the form of a teaching dialogue, revealed through questions and answers between the resurrected Jesus and his closest disciples, during which the disciples frequently quote from the Psalms to introduce their responses. Four out of the eleven disciples are female and the number of declaratory statements made by them is very revealing. Where Peter and Andrew speak only five times each, Mary Magdalene speaks eighty-three times! When the twenty-six speeches of Sophia/Wisdom are added, the female role of language is more than three times that of the male. These statistics make it clear that the Pistis Sophia was created to restore the feminine energy stream to balance what was happening within Christianity at the time.

This motive is also made clear during the teaching dialogues when, on a number of occasions, Jesus tells the group that whatever they may think they understand about Mary Magdalene, she is no ordinary person, for she not only knows "the All" (the Source), but she is an earthly representative of the All. Reading this I was not surprised that she could fall into a trance on hearing the teachings of her soul mate, the resurrected Jesus, especially when he says that personal enlightenment is initiated by the feminine energies of the Source. Jesus's words in the Pistis Sophia were virtually identical to those in the Dialogue with the Savior.

Though it was created some eighteen centuries ago, the implications of the Pistis Sophia were pointing out the relevance of Maryam's words to me and renewing my optimism about her return to our life today. I had found clues supporting my strong feeling that after the Crucifixion, Maryam was the leader and primary teacher of the Jesus and Magdalene movement. Her qualifications for this role are confirmed by her displaying a spirituality and spiritual understanding far in advance of any of the other close disciples. Most striking are Jesus's statements about her being the embodiment of the All, pointing to his knowing that she was therefore the embodiment of Wisdom. The significance for the early Coptic church community was that Sophia/Wisdom was the consort of Jesus in the person of Mary Magdalene.

The idea of consort, of the other half of a sacred partnership, sounded very much like the wise, compassionate Maryam who had spoken to me some years earlier and the same amazing woman who graces the remaining pages of the Gospel of Mary. Moreover, I had also discovered the connection between the feminine energy known as Wisdom and the Mary Magdalene portrayed in the Faith of Wisdom story.

From ancient times shamanic teachers and prophets have favored authenticity and spontaneity. Maryam was one such teacher. The Gnostic texts tell how, because of her insistence on these two qualities as a marker of truth, she was seen by many of her companions, as well as Temple officials, as a threat to male religious authority. But she did not come to destroy the teachings of her ancestral spirituality, rather to embody the way of being to which they were moving, emphasizing that personal transformation was essential and that mere rote worship and prayer were pointless. She taught that as a manifestation of the divine, each of us has something unique to offer, for that is why we came here, as a facet of the Creator, like the rest of Creation.

I knew that the clues I had gathered to Maryam's identity sadly confirmed that her community would not be the one that later became the powerful, Roman-backed institution with which we are familiar. If this was so, apart from those suggested by the Gospel of Mary, had any of her teachings survived? My encounters with Maryam left me with a feeling that they had and that they might be hidden in another way. When I added this feeling to the revelations about her in the Gnostic texts, I was convinced that somewhere there was a story which would, like the cross on an ancient treasure map, mark the spot.

4

SEEKING THE
TREASURE MAP

One morning I was alerted by a remark made by a rabbi on breakfast radio. In his gentle, avuncular voice, he was saying: "Sacred books are like treasure maps, but you know, everyone's life is a sacred scripture, a treasure map showing the journey of the soul." I gulped down my coffee and made a note that sacred scriptures and sacred lives were treasure maps, in the hope that its meaning would later reveal itself. It was time to look at the New Testament material.

MARYAM,
ACCORDING TO THE NEW TESTAMENT

Christianity claims her, while at the same time it carefully rejects her. Having discovered the Maryam of the Nag Hammadi texts, I was surprised, but not put off, by the meager references to her in the four gospels of the New Testament. They may be the earliest surviving records about Maryam, but they might contain clues to the church's ambivalence about her. I knew they were written by men within a patriarchal society that found it difficult to even contemplate, let alone accept, women as complementary human beings, equal to men. History is written by those in power at the time so it seems highly likely that these canonical records have been edited according to a specific patriarchal and dogmatic agenda.

This was the backdrop to the historical figure of Mary Magdalene, but I was sure that its very emptiness pointed to something that had remained purposely overlooked. When such a gap is left in what has been accepted for centuries, I don't just wonder why, but what if? Clues to how and why her memory has survived in spite of the limited, negative references to her are, of course, in the so-called Gnostic material in which she is a very important central character.

Toward the end of the first century, church theologians began to monitor the teachings of the various groups with a view to bringing them under a central governing body. In 180 CE the champion of orthodoxy, Bishop Irenaeus of Lyons, set out a canon in which the Jewish scriptures were named the Old Testament. What came after would be the New Testament, to include the four gospels Matthew, Mark, Luke, and John. The Bishop's reasoning was that there were four directions, four oceans, and four corners of the world; therefore, it was divinely ordained that there must be four gospels. Even so, heated debates about what Yeshua taught and what he actually meant continued. This situation persisted for another hundred years, but conflicting versions of the teachings did not appeal to the Roman need for order and control.

The emerging church, however, now clearly run along institutional lines, did appeal to the Romans. Emperor Constantine saw an opportunity to unite the increasingly divided empire by declaring Christianity as the only state religion. In 325 CE he convened a council at Nicaea (now Iznik in Turkey) with a view to systematizing the writings according to an agreed doctrine. After protracted and often brutal arguments, the outcome was the selection of the twenty-seven items originally approved by Irenaeus. So it was decreed that Jesus, as "the Christ," was not simply a spiritual master, but synonymous with the one and only true God. This meant that humans could find salvation from a life of sin through Jesus Christ alone. Further, the new religion made it clear that Christian belief was essential since everyone was born a sinner.

There was now only one acceptable canon of the Christian religion. All other writings, viewpoints, and opinions about Yeshua and Christian doctrine would be considered heretical (including his Hebrew name), and heresy could be punishable by death. The rule of Roman orthodoxy was assured.

The four approved gospels had been compiled in the second half of the first century CE and, as part of the oral tradition, were intended to be read aloud. New recruits to the Roman institution of Christianity would have wondered how a righteous man, declared the savior of all, came to be executed by the Romans. This may have been why the first gospel, Mark, includes a detailed account of the arrest, trial, and execution of Yeshua, with Jewish betrayers and priests, rather than Romans, portrayed as the real villains. The Gospel of Matthew fills out Mark's narrative, but addresses the Judean audience. Luke also seems to have borrowed material from Mark and is thought to address a Samaritan and cosmopolitan Galilean audience.

The one thing the four gospels had in common was a record of the Crucifixion and Resurrection. After Yeshua's arrest the male disciples had fled, though a group of women remained at the site until Yeshua was taken down from the cross and they later discovered the empty tomb and the "risen" Yeshua. Each gospel names different women, but only Maryam features in all four accounts. John goes further to say that she is the first and lone witness to the empty tomb and then to the risen Yeshua (20:1–18). The Luke narrative confirms the prejudices of the time, for when the women tell the rest of the disciples about their experience, they are ridiculed and not believed (24:10–11).

News of Maryam's encounter with the risen Yeshua must have spread so rapidly that many soon knew about it. Perhaps that was why the gospel writers could not cover up the incident and keep her out of the story. Much later the church announced that this made her the "Apostle to the Apostles," but the title suggests more than simply being the first witness to something special. I felt that there was a reason why she was described as the first witness, and the gospel writers weren't telling us.

The John depiction of Maryam made me wonder if there were more clues about her. I was struck by the emphasis in this gospel on beginnings and rebirths and repeated references by Yeshua to the "I AM" (one of the ancient Jewish names of the Source). The Seven Signs, or "miracles," aroused my curiosity because for Jews it is the sacred number of completion. The more I studied this gospel, the more I heard Maryam's voice, urging me to "look behind the words of the story."

In what is thought to be the original last chapter of the Fourth Gospel (chapter 20), the redactor has left another clue to the beloved Maryam. She is standing distraught outside the empty tomb, wondering what has become of Yeshua's body, when he shows himself to her in his subtle body. However, she does not recognize him. The subtle energy body is the one we remain in immediately after passing out of the physical. Though visible to clairvoyant vision, it is not visible to normal everyday sight. Yeshua's subtle body, now appearing as if filled with light, would have looked very different to the beaten and tortured frame she had seen some hours earlier. No wonder she failed to recognize him.

But when Yeshua calls Maryam by her name, she realizes who he is, crying: "Rabbuni!" ("my dear Teacher"). In a rush of grief and excitement, she reaches out to embrace him, giving rise to the well-known, and well-misunderstood, Latin phrase: *noli me tangere*. In Jewish culture only a wife would touch a man in this way. Yeshua is saying "Don't try to grab hold of me" for two reasons. First, she must have been used to this instinctive act of intimacy; and second, he was no longer in his physical body so she would pass straight through him! Yeshua uses his spiritual power to show that a person survives after death, and his beloved Maryam is the first person to witness this.

Here, the whole point of the Resurrection is revealed. Being able to show the subtle body to another proves that Yeshua was a great spiritual master, but much more importantly it proves the survival of the soul after the death of the body. Yeshua is dramatically proclaiming that there is no death! This has been tragically missed by Christianity in its need to make Jesus the Godman and the only person with the power to physically rise from the dead. Maryam did have clairvoyant vision. If this was her record of events, it makes sense, but if it was John's, how did he know about such an intimate encounter?

DRAWING ASIDE THE VEILS

Continuing the detective work, I came to realize that the way something is put often points to a veil that, when drawn aside, reveals yet further clues. In the Gospel of John, one of these veils is a certain woman named Mary who behaves in a singular way. Mary has a sister, Martha, and a brother, Lazarus, and they live together in the village of Bethany. The family is well known for its support of Yeshua and his movement.

One day Lazarus falls critically ill and Martha rushes to ask Yeshua to come and save him from death's door. Strangely, Yeshua waits a few days but eventually sets off for Bethany. As he approaches the house, Martha goes out to meet him, but Mary stays in the house. This was the normal behavior of a Jewish wife, not a friendly supporter. Martha goes back indoors and whispers to her sister: "The Rabbi is here and is calling for you!" Hearing this Mary jumps up and quickly goes to him (10:28–29). Again, this is the behavior of a wife being summoned by her husband. This is the same Mary, John tells us in advance, who "anointed the Lord with perfume and wiped his feet with her hair." So do we need to know this about her before we come to the actual account, or is it an echo of something already known to the listener from another source?

Sure enough, in the next chapter Yeshua calls by to see how Lazarus is getting on after being "raised from the dead." As Yeshua is sitting at dinner with the disciples, Mary pours a pound of costly spikenard oil over his feet and wipes them with her hair. These astounding actions could only have been performed by a woman who was both known to and intimate with Yeshua. This might well have caused uproar among the male disciples, but, interestingly, only Judas expresses anger at what he sees as a waste of money—a year's wages for a laborer. Again, John tells us in advance that this is the man who will betray Yeshua. Yeshua calms Judas down, telling the gathering that she had bought it to keep for the day of his burial (12:7).

So John gives us a picture of a Mary who not only behaves like a wife, and is intimate like a wife, but obviously understands something about Yeshua that the others do not. Did Yeshua already know about Mary's expensive purchase or was it his powers of clairvoyance? I began to wonder if this couple had planned the purchase together.

The Mark gospel also records this landmark event. However, in his account an unnamed woman comes in, apparently unannounced, and, like the anointing of a king, pours the spikenard oil over Yeshua's *head*. Again, there is uproar and Yeshua declares that the anointing is preparation for his burial, and furthermore, the woman would always be remembered for her beautiful act—as an anonymous, unknown woman! This incident also takes place at Bethany "at the house of Simon the leper" (14:3). Curiously, the Dead Sea Scrolls indicate that Bethany was the name of a leper colony, yet Lazarus, Martha, and Mary lived there too. We may wonder what they and Yeshua were doing there since Jewish law prohibited contact with lepers.

Luke also writes about the two sisters, but is careful to say that they lived in "a certain village." In his account, when the wandering group calls by, Martha busies herself in the kitchen, but Mary sits at Yeshua's feet to listen to him. When Martha complains that Mary is not helping her, he remarks that she is worried and distracted and would be better off emulating her sister Mary. Mary has chosen the one thing that is necessary, he says, and this will not be taken away from her (10:38–42). Luke does not mention anything about spikenard, yet this was obviously an event that caused quite a stir with the inner group of followers.

All three gospels leave us with interesting questions. Who is this "Mary"? If she was simply one of the many females who supported the

Yeshua movement, how did she ever think it was appropriate to touch him, let alone anoint him? How did she come to have an expensive quantity of spikenard oil, and why did she pour the whole lot over him? This Mary acts in ways that anyone of the time would have recognized as only appropriate for a *wife*. But, like the unnamed woman, she also knew something about Yeshua that the other disciples clearly did not. She is an avid follower, yet Mary of Bethany does not appear in the Crucifixion and Resurrection scenes.

This evidence suggests that Mary of Bethany was the same person as Maryam. Indeed, the Gospel of John gives an important clue in the Lazarus story. When Martha rushes indoors to her sister, she says: "The Rabbi is calling for you." She does not call him lord, or savior, or messiah. As we saw earlier in the Resurrection scene, when Yeshua calls Maryam by her name, she responds with the intimate and affectionate title that she had always used: Rabbuni. For centuries the church was at pains to keep Mary of Bethany and Mary the Magdalene separate, though now many concede that they are the same person.

But in case we get too carried away with this new vision of Maryam, we are left with Luke's little aside—this was the woman who had been cleansed of seven demons (8:2). Luke's motive for being so dramatic may have been entirely different from the accepted tradition that she was in a very bad mental state. Other women in the group had been healed of various infirmities, but, for some reason, Maryam is named and her condition is specifically described. Here again, seven, the sacred number of completion, features. Is the story really saying that Maryam was someone special and that she had been made complete, in the sense of whole? The seven subtle energy centers (chakras), that provide the vital link between our physical being and the subtle and spiritual levels, were known to Jewish and Middle Eastern mystics. I think it is very possible that Maryam had been through a special ceremony in which she had been balanced and harmonized on all seven levels—she was complete. This rare state would have been a necessary preparation for her role as *complement* to Yeshua. Or perhaps an original version of Luke was actually commenting on Maryam's unusual spiritual development. Luke does not make it clear, but the hint is that Yeshua was the powerful healer and holy man concerned.

After her crucial role at the Resurrection, Maryam, as a named person, disappears from the canonical story of the Yeshua movement, and there is no explanation for this. One possibility is that if she had become the natural successor to Yeshua, and continued teaching, she would have been a threat to the misogynistic Christianity of the Peter and Paul groups. Their teachings gained the approval of the church and the Roman state. The need to maintain their patriarchal power base meant that any reference to Mary Magdalene as equal with, or successor to, Yeshua would have to be deleted. In doing so they committed the greater tragedy for humans by suppressing the sacred feminine and deleting the eternal message: "You are all Christs, or Christs in the making."

At this point in the investigations, my image of Maryam was becoming fuller and clearer. Even if I ignored the evidence in the Nag Hammadi scriptures, the canonical material shows that as well as being on intimate terms with Yeshua, Maryam behaves very much like his admiring wife and seems to have greater spiritual insight about him than the closest disciples. She also took a leading role in some key episodes of Yeshua's life. The spiritual standing given to her by the church apparently derives from the John account of her being the first witness to the Resurrection. But the hints and allusions found in three of the gospels show that to both Yeshua and the disciples, she was someone special *before* that event. I felt that I was getting close to realizing the church's motive for playing down her spiritual eminence. I was also discovering more evidence to back up the theory of a Magdalene community and Magdalene teachings that may even have later been committed to writing.

MARYAM THE COMPANION

The thorough and ruthless attempts to erase the sacred feminine failed. From the time of the Crucifixion, stories about Maryam and her teachings abounded, and traditions grew up in the Middle East and later in southern Europe that have stood the test of time, denigration, and the Inquisition. If she had been nothing more than a supporter of the Jesus movement, her memory would have remained minimal. Instead it has grown. Now, in our own time, millennia later, she enters our consciousness again with even greater spiritual power.

This force reveals long-buried truths and raises consciousness in individual lives through a series of awakenings. I can now see that the awakening I experienced at the cave of Sainte Baume was part of such a series, and I am sure that the Magdalene awakenings have a pattern for all who are touched by them. As you read these words, perhaps you are aware of one or more awakening experiences, in the sense that now, as you look back, you can see how Maryam—or a similar "feminine" spiritual force—has been your companion and your initiator. She will have taken you from one awakening to another until the urgency and truth of her message dawned on you. Like so many of my own, most of your awakenings probably happened without any reference to her. Yet now you find that they have led you to the Magdalene energy stream. Maryam has entered our consciousness because we are ready to receive her—energetically and spiritually. This time of spiritual readiness is the outcome of energies that were unleashed centuries ago. These energies exerted a creative force that provided the opportunities for discovery and revelation, and the discoveries point to those parts of the Middle East where Maryam was once greatly revered.

Having studied the books of the New Testament carefully, I sat and thought about the remarks made by the radio rabbi. The only text that felt anything like a treasure map was the Fourth Gospel, the Gospel of John. I read through the passages about "Mary" again. On the surface the gospel was another member of the Christian canon with scant references to Mary Magdalene, though, for some reason, toward the end of the gospel, the writer had mentioned her ability to see Jesus in his spirit body after the Crucifixion. This tallied very nicely with the Gnostic descriptions of Maryam as a visionary able to receive important teachings from Jesus after his death.

DID MARYAM
WRITE THE FOURTH GOSPEL?

At the end of a long evening of study, I looked up from a pile of research papers, aware that my hand was over my heart to ease an ache in the chest and with goose bumps on my skin. Mary Magdalene was the author of the Fourth Gospel, not some guy called John or even Yokhanan, of this I was quite certain. Now I would have to find the clues that would reveal the feminine energy that created the work, and the source of this energy, who I knew as Maryam—Mary Magdalene.

In 1993 Margaret Starbird's *The Woman With The Alabaster Jar* startled Christians all over the planet and encouraged those demanding an equal and feminine voice in the church. Starbird, as a practicing Catholic, had come to the troubling realization that Mary Magdalene must have been married to Jesus because no woman who was not already his wife would have been allowed to touch him, let alone anoint him with costly spikenard oil. Her research led her to another troubling conclusion that Mary Magdalene had been marginalized and then denigrated to bolster the patriarchal misogynous culture of the church, thereby denying all Christians a great gift—the wisdom and beauty of the feminine. It seemed that Starbird's book had begun the process of preparing the world for the advent of Mary Magdalene consciousness and the reintegration of the feminine energy stream into human life. Just as the Gnostic texts had indicated, Maryam was indeed the Beloved Disciple, not a young man named John.

WHAT'S IN A NAME?

In the gospels she is more than a "Mary," singled out by an epithet that still baffles the pundits. In Greek her name has been written as Maria i Magdalini, "Mary the Magdalene." But so far no record has been found of what they were translating. When the Greek scribe had to translate the Hebrew name Yehuda ish Qariot—"The Jewish man from Qariot"— he came up with Judas Iscariot, so the assumption has always been that i Magdalini was descriptive in some way. Some authors maintain that she was named after the important Galilean fishing town of Magdala. If so, the significance of that name is still a matter of speculation. The Greek title is probably a translation of that used by her own followers— the Magdal-eder—after the stone tower used by shepherds to watch over their flocks. Margaret Starbird suggests that her epithet may have been used to echo the prophetic words of the shaman-priest Micah: "And you, O tower of the flock, O stronghold of the daughter of Zion, to you it shall come, the former dominion shall come, the sovereignty of daughter Jerusalem" (Micah 4:8). This phrase would have resonated strongly with her followers, reminding them of their teacher Maryam.

In view of her advanced spirituality, the origin of her epithet seems more likely to have been derived from an understanding of the prophet Micah's declaration. As the Pistis Sophia and other Gnostic scriptures indicate, she could equally be addressed as Sofia. When Maryam said to me: "My name is Maryam" she did not bother with her epithet. This threw me back on my own intention. Did I want to get into a learned debate about her real name or did I want to experience her energy? Further, if I spent years looking into the legends, myths, opinions, and suppositions about her, would I be any the wiser? Like all the other controversies about her, the derivation of her title is another diversion from exploring the purpose of her once physical presence on planet Earth and her powerful spiritual presence in the consciousness of people today.

Three years after Starbird's bombshell book, fictional and academic books about Mary Magdalene were proliferating, with most of them missing the point of why she had come to our planet. Meanwhile, the controversial bishop John Shelby Spong continued his search for biblical truth with his *Liberating the Gospels: Reading the Bible with Jewish Eyes* in which he sought to "free Jesus from 2,000 years of misunderstanding." A Jewish perspective, he argues, shows that the three synoptic gospels—Matthew, Mark, and Luke—were each designed for a specific ethnic audience and structured to align with and overlay the Hebrew liturgical year. However, he was not so sure about the purpose of the fourth, or John, gospel. There was something about this gospel that was both cryptic and gloriously mysterious. He felt that the definitive work on the Fourth Gospel would not be written "until someone can place the book in its original Jewish setting, discover the motive and the agenda of its original Jewish author, and in this manner open the mysteries hidden away for so long." Even so he did not think there was one word in the text of this gospel that Jesus actually came close to saying.

Ah! Reading those words I felt I had intuited that the "treasure map" was hidden in the Fourth Gospel and it seemed that a prominent bishop, John Shelby Spong, had confirmed this for me.

MORE CONFIRMATION

Two more years of research went by when, in an Internet article, a Catholic scholar, Ramon K. Jusino, announced that he had also been studying the Fourth Gospel and had come to the conclusion that Mary Magdalene was both the Beloved Disciple and author of the gospel. In his article he carefully cites evidence to back up his claim. I was thrilled to have my own feelings confirmed by a committed Christian, but neither Starbird nor Jusino had managed to discover Bishop Spong's key factors of the original Jewish setting and the motive and agenda of its original Jewish author. This only encouraged me to push on with my own research. I thought back to my cave encounter with Maryam. "Look behind the words," she had said. "See the force behind the story."

Perhaps these words now illuminated the link between herself and my intuitive pursuit of the meaning behind the Fourth Gospel. There was some seemingly unknown force, the jeweled message, behind its story and this force was carefully encoded in the words of the story. The setting was there for all to see, but the motive and agenda of the author were yet to reveal themselves.

A NEW ENCOUNTER WITH MARYAM

With the success of my book *Hands-On Healing,* I was giving workshops both in the UK and abroad. It had become clear to me that many physical conditions had their origins in people's emotional and mental lives, and I was recommending that healers should study some form of counseling as a vital addition to their therapeutic work. In 1999 I took the opportunity to take a diploma course at Swansea University in art and person-centered counseling. We were encouraged to keep a visual as well as a written journal to record whatever was happening to us during the course. Mine turned out to be a kind of illustrated stream of consciousness.

A recurring journal image was a deserted beach with palm trees at either end. In one of these images, a huge open treasure chest stood at the top of the beach. But I did not make the connection with my childhood vision until a weekend workshop in London with the artist and writer Sue Michaelson. Sue also had a background in transpersonal psychology, and her method suited my diploma course perfectly. She used guided visualizations to initiate images from the subconscious that we would then try to illustrate. During one such visualization, I found myself looking at the same beach, but now the treasure chest was replaced by two golden-skinned, dark-haired women dancing together along the shore. One of the women was completely naked apart from a garland around her neck while the other was clothed in blue robes. Two thousand years ago, Miriam (Mary) was a Hebrew title given to priestesses, or female shamans, who were distinguished by their blue robes. I felt that I was seeing two versions of Maryam—one was her naked, true self and the other was completely clothed in the robes of myth and legend, and even lies, about her.

In a quiet little studio above a shop in London, that image was the breakthrough I had been working toward. By showing herself as naked, like the brown-skinned people in my childhood vision, Maryam helped me discover at last the connection between my beach vision and my cave encounter with her. But there was more. Back at Swansea University, I turned up the recurring course images of a beach and found the one with an open treasure chest. I gazed at it until I could see the sparkle of the jewels and the light emanating from the golden objects. I quickly made a new image in which the treasure chest becomes the Fourth Gospel as Maryam dances by along the sandy shore.

MARYAM'S MILLENNIUM AND *THE DA VINCI CODE*

On the eve of the new millennium (2000), I still felt the elation that my weekends in London had brought me to discovering what the treasure chest really had inside. The first BBC Television News of the year closed with a circular symbol under which were the Roman numerals for 2,000: MM. For many centuries the church owed its privilege and colossal power to the backing of the Roman state and used Latin as its sacred language. Many institutions, such as the BBC, have continued to use Roman numerals to indicate the year. It seemed a perfect irony to me that for a thousand years, the date would now begin with initials of Maryam's name. It was *her* millennium!

This change to the calendar seemed to increase the momentum of publications about Mary Magdalene. With his book, *The Da Vinci Code,* in 2003, Dan Brown, an American thriller writer who specializes in the cryptic, joined the library shelves now brimming with fiction and nonfiction about her. Acknowledging his debt to Margaret Starbird, Brown had cleverly developed the controversial theme about Maryam's alleged marriage to Jesus, her pregnancy, and the resulting bloodline, which, in 1996, had been described by Laurence Gardner and others as the Holy Grail. In spite of its many inaccuracies, *The Da Vinci Code,* followed by a film based on the book, proved a worldwide success and stirred up further interest in the Magdalene story. The popular focus on Maryam's possible escape to Gaul, pregnant with Jesus's baby daughter, did little to help us understand why she was suddenly in the news and the focus for both veneration and speculation. Nevertheless I surmised that as with Starbird's work, the *The Da Vinci Code* was another step toward preparing the world for the full force of Maryam's energy stream. I saw the growing interest in her as evidence that she had penetrated the human psyche.

5
FINDING THE
TREASURE CHEST

Every great teacher has a story to tell. Two thousand years ago Jesus and Mary Magdalene came to planet Earth with a thrilling story, with images that are still fresh and revolutionary today. Theirs is a love story about Oneness—their oneness with each other, their oneness with us, our oneness with each other, our oneness with all that is, and our oneness with the Source. Maryam and Yeshua were a very special partnership that demonstrated the equality and unity of masculine and feminine and the power generated when these two energy streams were combined—a demonstration that the male disciples of the time were reluctant to admit and which the church that they founded took desperate measures to erase. A great gift was denied and human beings have suffered the consequences ever since.

THE GOSPEL OF SIGNS IS
MARYAM'S TEACHING STORY

The Nag Hammadi evidence suggests that after the death of her beloved and best friend, Maryam found that the way to deal with her grief and heartbreak was to continue the work that she and Yeshua had begun together. I guessed that like any spiritual teacher of the time, she would have taught through stories that were delivered orally. Dramatic stories are the most easily remembered, making them the ideal teaching form. I felt sure that Maryam's dramatic stories would be the treasures in the chest of the Fourth Gospel. It was her presence that had made it the strange, mystical document that it still is, in spite of the alterations that have been made to it. *She* was the guiding spirit, not those who later committed her teachings to writing. It was time to look behind the words at the force of the story, *her* story.

In their original written form, the gospels were not divided into chapters and even the meaning of words had to be guessed from the sense of the narrative. Later translators separated the material into chapters and verses to make the gospels easier to read. With this division, the first eleven chapters of the John gospel make a satisfying whole. Some scholars have even named them the Gospel of Signs because they present a carefully structured series of seven events, involving Jesus as shaman-healer, described by the storyteller as "signs." In Christian dogma the seven miracle stories, featuring Jesus as a wonder-worker, are the signs that point to him as divine messiah. However, his message was that each person was a divine soul with a physical body. Maryam had confirmed this to me when she said that everyone was a Christ or in the process of becoming one.

If healings and miraculous happenings were the order of the day in the Palestine of Yeshua's time, with wonder-workers in every town and village, then the Seven Signs must be pointing to something else. Perhaps this something else was about everyone being a messiah, an anointed one. Perhaps "a Christ in the making" was a person in the process of coming to that inner realization. I did not have the answers, but I began to wonder if the message of the signs was not trapped but, like the Gnostic texts, had been skillfully hidden or disguised as a series of episodes in a highly dramatic story, the story known as the Gospel of Signs.

HOW THE FOURTH GOSPEL CAME TO BE

The Fourth Gospel has its own history. I wondered if somewhere in the life of this text, there were clues about its meaning. With Jewish unrest and Roman oppression, the Palestine in which it was conceived was often chaotic and dangerous. History shows that living on the edge breeds both radical new ideas and open-minded thinking, with the courage to explore and embrace them. I guessed this was why the souls of Maryam and Yeshua chose to incarnate at that crossroads of time and place. They were living on the edge.

From 50 BCE onward, radical versions of Judaism abounded, of which the Jesus and Mary Magdalene movement is perhaps the best known. Then, around 30 CE, there were big changes when Yeshua was executed by the Roman occupiers. As the political situation in Palestine began to deteriorate further, Maryam continued to teach, but without the commanding presence of Yeshua, the patriarchal misogyny within Judaism emerged once more as male members of the movement threatened to go their own way. By this time, already facing discrimination from other Hebrews as well as breakaway groups of mainly male followers, it is thought that the Magdalene community decided to preserve her teachings by writing them down in Aramaic.

Authorities such as Raymond Brown suggest that the main breakaway group, under the leadership of Peter and Andrew, took copies of these written teachings with them. Appearing on the surface to be stories about Jesus, they could easily be adapted and redacted to create a "gospel" in accordance with the dogma developing in the emergent Christian church.

Then, in a bid to ensure their survival, the gospel was translated into Greek. With his new name and title of Yesous Khristos—Jesus Christ—Yeshua was effectively gentile-ized, allowing those who had left Mary Magdalene to divorce themselves from their Semitic roots. With the combined threats of Roman and orthodox Jewish persecution, the smaller Jewish spiritual groups either went underground or left Palestine altogether. This included the Galilean group that had remained loyal to Maryam, the Beloved Disciple.

In 70 CE the Romans finally put an end to continuous Jewish revolts by destroying the Jerusalem Temple and massacring the Jewish population. At about the same time, the Greek version of the gospel was completed somewhere outside Palestine. Unlike the three synoptic gospels, no one could come up with a credible name for Maryam's redacted teachings. It was simply known as the *Fourth Gospel*. Decades went by until the notorious heresy-hunter and creator of the Christian canon, Bishop Irenaeus (ca. 125–ca. 202 CE), said he had overheard his old mentor, Bishop Polycarp of Smyrna, say that the gospel had been written by the apostle John. Moreover, this John was none other than "the beloved disciple" mentioned in the gospel. The new gospel was therefore christened "According to John."

Its contents did not quite gel with what Matthew, Mark, and Luke had to say, and many authorities in the new church felt that it had a disturbing similarity to some of the heretical Gnostic texts. As I had discovered, for over a century its element of mystery perplexed quite a few bishops until, after some considerable wrangling at the Council of Nicaea in 325 CE, it was officially made part of the canon of approved Christian texts. By then Maryam's original purpose in creating the stories that appear in the Gospel of John had long been completely obscured and morphed into a dogmatic form of Christology. Today, claims and controversy still surround the Fourth Gospel as academics and biblical pundits attempt to unravel its mysteries. Who actually wrote it? Where and when was it written? Why is it so different from the other three? What is it really about? Why is it so Jewish? And who really was the beloved disciple?

It seemed to me that the historical perspective revealed that any teacher, such as Maryam, would have had a very good reason to encode her message, especially if that message challenged current religious orthodoxy. But a lesson in history had not brought me any closer to "opening the mysteries hidden away for so long." The words of John

Shelby Spong about the need for a totally new approach to the Fourth Gospel seemed to be the key. In Maryam's Teaching Story, the Jewish setting is in the Palestine that her followers would recognize, with its biblical references and specifically Jewish calendar. Her motive was to help people raise their consciousness to experience the presence of the Source, poetically described as "entering the Kingdom." But her agenda could not be made too obvious, and so I surmised that it was encoded in the Teaching Story.

SETTING OUT THE SEVEN SIGNS

To get some clarity, my search beneath the surface of the story began by setting out the seven healing events. The story is introduced with some careful remarks about its dreamlike context. We are at the beginning of something, in a time past that is simultaneously time present, on the east bank of the River Jordan, near the village of Bethany, before Yeshua had become well known. At first there is a hint that the story could be about the journeying soul, like the journey of Sophia/Wisdom in the Pistis Sophia, but the hint quickly gives way to a picture of the first character Yokhanan (John) who is immersing people in the river waters—a typical Jewish preparation ritual. Then the main character, Yeshua, appears and is briefly fleshed out through some encounters with named people who will become his followers. The parameters of the story are now in place. What follows are the seven significant events—the Signs—involving the healing powers of Yeshua, as he and his companions travel back and forth from the Jordan to the Galilee, and the city of Jerusalem, via Samaria.

In Sign One water is turned into wine at a wedding (John 2). Sign Two describes how an official's sick child recovers through distant healing (John 4). In Sign Three a man is healed and walks again after being paralyzed for thirty-eight years (John 5). During Sign Four a large crowd is fed with only five loaves and two fishes (John 6). Sign Five is either about Yeshua calming a storm or appearing to walk on water, or both (John 6). In Sign Six a man blind from birth recovers his sight when Yeshua spits on clay dirt and applies the paste to the man's eyes (John 9). I made a note here that since it was about seeing with new eyes, the recovery of sight through a shamanic healing act might be a pivotal metaphor in the story. Finally, in Sign Seven a man thought to be dead walks from his burial tomb and throws off his burial cloths at Yeshua's command (John 11).

Sign Seven brings Yeshua and his party back to where the story started, near the village of Bethany. This circular element is a typical feature of Semitic teaching, where the listener/reader is taken back to the starting point of the story, only to find that the original situation has changed and that he have also been changed by his experience of the story. If Maryam was the teacher behind the Teaching Story, just like other spiritual teachers of the time, her method would have been oral. Someone else would have made a note of her teachings and later written them down. Looking at the circular structure of the Seven Signs, it now looked very probable that the Gospel of Signs was actually a dramatic and colorful Teaching Story and that Mary Magdalene was the teacher.

THE SEMITIC WAY OF KNOWING

The primary mode of cognition that dominates our culture, and favored by scientists during the past few centuries, has been its tendency toward linear analysis, reductionism, and an insistence on the mechanical nature of the natural world. I learned this way of operating from age thirteen, but I began to see its drawbacks when I came to work with farm animals, the land, and the British climate. There was something almost magical about these aspects of Nature that my scientific training could not help me grasp. I sensed that there must be another way of approaching the world. Years later a Native American teacher showed me that there was another mode of cognition, tried and tested by ancient and indigenous cultures, that is holistic and intuitive and in which the heart rather than the brain is the organ of perception. For example, I learned that any part of Nature can speak to us, whether animal, plant, rock, river, landscape, or climate, and we can hear what Nature has to say once we have developed deep and attentive listening as part of training ourselves in perceiving with the heart. This method of knowing is much more than a way of gathering knowledge. It is a way of being.

The ancient Semitic way of being was very similar in that it saw no division between a person's inner and outer life and that the heavenly and the earthly were one continuum. This holistic perception of life encouraged people to see more than its surface, to hear what lay behind a person's words, and to be aware of what generated their actions. The words of a spiritual teacher, whether spoken or written down, were thought to have a special energy with the power to transform the listener or reader. Moreover, the magic of the teacher's delivery meant that every individual listener or reader would perceive the words at the level of their own understanding. This is hinted at in the Gospel of Philip where Yeshua reminds his followers that you can only understand a spiritual concept when you have the same consciousness as that reality (61:20). In other words relax and go with whatever resonates for you.

I felt that in spite of whatever had happened to her original words, the beautiful jewel of their message had become crystallized, trapped in the rocky strata of out-of-date dogma and the theological battles of senile fanatics, and I could still trust their power to guide me to her teaching agenda. Next I needed to find some way of extracting the jewel.

FROM MIDRASH TO MEANING

As Spong had intuited, I needed to approach the Gospel of Signs with the heart as organ of perception. With this in mind, I decided to approach the text through the Semitic way of interpretation, or *midrash*. Here, when confronted by a sacred text, the listener or reader is encouraged to plunge into the words, and the *atmosphere* of the words, to discover their meaning. Midrash, from the Hebrew verb meaning "to search out," is a process of reading between the lines of an ancient story. This method may fill in pieces that seem to be missing, give new life to outdated forms, bring fresh understanding, or even reveal a hidden mystery. Such imaginative searches do not invalidate the ancient stories or replace them; rather, they provide a bridge between the people of now and the people of then, giving an ancient message a contemporary and relevant reality. A vital aspect of the technique is meditation before, during, or after working with a text; it is important to listen to the heart and feel what the need of the moment is.

It was a case of total immersion, swimming in the words and images and wrestling with their implications, absorbing the feelings that they created, and all the time wondering what the text really meant, what it really wanted to say.

HEALING THE WORLD
MEANS HEALING OURSELVES

The ancient holistic-intuitive way of approaching a sacred text can be applied to anything in your life since it arises directly from our interconnectedness with and interdependence on all the life that surrounds us. From ancient times this Semitic worldview also assumes two sacred responsibilities: healing the world and healing the individual. Because every individual journey is an integral part of the life journey of all beings, the journey of our planet, and the whole universe, each person has the sacred responsibility to engage in the healing of the world. In our time there have been calls to become more aware of the human exploitation of planetary resources and to repair the damage already done to the planet. Other voices point out that our planet is quite capable of healing itself so that human responsibility is about our attitude to the Earth and the way we treat its gifts. Thus the phrase points to a deeper understanding. Healing the world means healing our *relationship* with the world. It is our relationship that needs to be repaired. But experience tells us that healing relationships calls for inner change—we will need to change. Now the second sacred responsibility becomes apparent—the healing of the individual self, in other words, the healing of our relationship with self.

Healing the world therefore depends upon the healing and transformation of each person. In their deepest sense, both meanings of repair (*tikkun* in Hebrew) are talking about an inner, personal change in our alignment with the sacred. When we realize that each person is sacred and that the planet and the whole world of Nature are sacred, we are healing our relationship with these aspects of Creation. Maryam's Teaching Story shows us how to achieve these realizations and healings through the progressive removal of our clouded vision. How does Maryam's Teaching Story do this?

THE STORY AND YOU

Like her spiritual partner Yeshua, Maryam never simply *preached* change. All the sacred texts that feature her indicate that she knew a change in human life would only come about through a new sensitivity, a new awareness, and a new understanding that could only arise through actually living a heart-centered approach to life. Her teaching was oral. You listened as carefully as you could and put into practice what you could. There were many advantages of being with a group of like-minded people (*khaverim* in Hebrew), such as sharing and comparing and having the support of the group.

I mentioned earlier how, in the ancient Semitic world, the teachings of a shaman-prophet were so revered that they were often written down by the special few who knew how to write. However, at first sight, those texts that have survived the ravages of time hardly seem like the how-to-do-it manuals or self-help books that we would recognize today. They seem more like stories, with asides that often led the storyteller to develop a parallel or totally different theme—rather like listening to a charismatic narrator round a campfire at night. In an orally-based world, a story, like a song, remains in the mind of the listener, and the story, like the song, always resonates in a way particular for each individual. The listener makes of the story what she will, and some of those listeners were the very people who later wrote down what they thought they heard and saw and sensed.

With these considerations in mind, we can be aware that the storytelling way of teaching does involve a kind of code—including an array of symbols and knowledge of ancient myths and stories, held together with poetic wordplay. Listeners at the time of the teachings had the extra advantage of seeing the teacher, hearing her voice, and observing her body language. Later readers had to rely on the text alone to guide them through the coded material. In our time, two millennia on, to crack the code like the listener/readers of old, it will not be enough to merely absorb the written words of Maryam's teachings. We will have to enter into the energetic atmosphere of each episode of the Story and feel what it has to say to us. When we let this happen, we allow the teachings to progressively change our consciousness so that we begin to notice how our behaviors, what we say, even our very thought patterns, are changing—we are becoming more heart-centered. We are cracking the code. A summary at the end of each chapter helps you assess your progress in this endeavor.

THE VALUE OF THE DREAM

So now comes the creative part. One way to work with Maryam's Teaching Story is to encounter the Gospel of Signs as you would a dream and pay attention to what follows. As Carl Jung emphasized, dreams are a valuable and also real part of human life. The dream world is a parallel world where anything is possible. Things that happen in the dream state may seem surreal when we experience them again with daytime consciousness. But it is the very possibility of the revelatory power of the surreal that makes the dream world a good companion on our pilgrim way. In dreams we meet the unexpected as if it is the norm. A second creative aspect of the dream state is to observe and enjoy your own dreams while you are working with Maryam's Teaching Story.

As a unique individual, you are going to devise your own ways of putting Maryam's teachings into practice. By all means find some like-minded friends who want to join you. They are unique individuals too. You will be working with the book in your way, and so will they. The outcomes belong to all of you.

PART TWO

The Way Through

Maryam's Teachings in
the Gospel of Signs

6

INTO
THE ORCHARD

Maryam's caution to "look behind the words" points out that through-out your quest, you will find that meaning has many levels and many facets. Indeed, the people of each generation need to interpret a sacred text in relation to their own times and conditions.

I mentioned how I had arrived at deciphering Maryam's encoded teachings by using midrash, a traditional Semitic method of interpret-ing and appreciating a sacred text. As a reader or listener, the seeker approaches a text as if it is a living organism, with respect and a sense of wonder. The method is carried out as a spiritual exercise, preceded by prayer, contemplation, and, above all, meditation, and often accompa-nied by other ways of focusing awareness, such as lighting candles and incense, chanting, and breathing exercises. This procedure is the secret of midrash, and its unique approach is known as entering the orchard (*pardes* in Hebrew). The letters PRDS indicate the four levels of mean-ing that a text might reveal—*peshat:* the simple, literal, or superficial meaning; *remez:* the meaning hinted at, or implied, through metaphor, allegory, poetry, parable, and dream; *derash:* the creative search for mean-ing, through interpretation, and even through what is felt intuitively; and *sod:* the most elusive, hidden, mystical, or transpersonal meaning.

To present Maryam's teachings I will be following this four-layered structure. The NRSV biblical text herein (see Suggestions for Further

Reading) is an example of the final redaction and edit of Maryam's words and represents level one: the literal meaning. We then plunge into the text to become more familiar with it, taking in relevant asides as we go along. This material is further enriched and expanded with the Gnostic and Nag Hammadi perspective outlined earlier. We can then appreciate the deeper, original message of the text, with its power to transform lives and situations. Try looking for your own meanings at the different levels.

When studying any ancient text, the important thing to remember is that your mind can only compare information and experiences with what is *already* in its database. For this reason I have found it essential, throughout the whole detection process, to keep an open mind, to take time out and be relaxed with multilayered meanings, trying to remain heart-based and see what resonates.

THE CORE THEME
OF MARYAM'S TEACHINGS

During Maryam's lifetime the people of Palestine were suffering from Roman oppression, but at a deeper level, human beings in general were suffering from the disastrous effects of disharmony and imbalance between the masculine and feminine energy streams, a primary wound arising from disconnection from the sacred. Two thousand years later finds the world in a similar state. This is what makes Maryam's teachings so relevant for our times. Her counsel is to clear our "clouded vision," the source of all our wounds of disconnection from the sacred, so clearly illustrated in the story of the Seven Signs. Once cleared, we realize that the central theme of all Maryam's teachings is to become heart-centered. Our thoughts, words, and behaviors become love-based, and the soul, rather than the mind and ego, is then free to express our sacred self, to guide us and help solve all our problems. Look out for the different ways in which Maryam's Teaching Story approaches this theme.

A text is always more than what we hear or read. I found that I could enter "the orchard" and enjoy its fruits by first treating the sacred texts I have mentioned as living things. By directly encountering the text through the holistic-intuitive method, by dialoguing with it, you can *experience* its meaning.

In 2009, during the Nobel Academy award to Italian writer Dario Fo, Salman Rushdie was invited to address the audience. He reminded them that only those who can tell their stories are free. I wonder if those who can really listen to and experience a story are equally free. If you follow Maryam's Teaching Story to its conclusion, you will have your answer.

SEVEN KEY STEPS TO TRANSFORMATION AND A CHANGE OF CONSCIOUSNESS

The key steps are revealed one by one as you make your way through the Seven Signs, each experience, understanding, and insight building on what has gone before. Working with the key steps in that order will lead you to develop the heart-centered approach to life that, in Maryam's teaching, is the purpose of personal transformation. At the same time you will begin to experience the change of consciousness and awareness that will lead to healing the Earth, for with each new awakening, we become progressively aware of the sacred nature of the planet and all its inhabitants.

A change in personal consciousness can affect other people, the planet, and the other planetary beings: simply recall that all is energy. Whether consciously or unconsciously, whatever our energetic state, we give out our energies to the world—first as a general energetic emanation, then as thought, as breath, as actions. At every moment we are having an energetic effect on others and the world. In this way, as they come into contact with us, the energy of others may be changed, the energy of the environment changes, and like ripples on a pool, the effect moves out into the world to encourage further change. This process is enhanced when a person raises her consciousness, or transforms, because her energy not only changes but her energy field expands. The effects of our energetic state on other people, and the world around us, may have been described in a two-thousand-year-old language picture, but this is exactly what the teachings and role models of both Yeshua and Maryam demonstrated.

THE METAPHOR OF THE SEVEN SIGNS

Yeshua operated in the same way as the Lakota holy man Fools Crow (ca.1890–1989) who taught that the purpose of healing was to reassure the community that the spiritual level of being was real and that the Source was with them. Jesus and Mary Magdalene did not come to perform miracles to overawe people into bowing down and treating them as gods. When we look deeper, the Seven Signs are not the signs that tell us Yeshua is a god or great being. Ending in seven, the number of completion, they are a metaphor for any person's spiritual journey and they tell us that each person is divine. As long as we continue to believe that the truths of spirituality are about someone else, about Yeshua, about Maryam, or about great shamanic healers, for example, we will miss the essential point about who we, as individuals, really are. Yeshua was not a Christian and neither was Mary Magdalene. Early Christianity formed its identity by ignoring Yeshua's revelation that the divine was in everyone and by disparaging Jews and women. At the conjunction of this triple repression are the experience and teachings of Mary Magdalene.

Maryam's path to healing consciousness is open and inclusive, and it may be traveled by anyone of any or no religion. We need only open our hearts and minds to the wisdom surrounding us at every moment and in every place, for healing consciousness is a state of awareness where the levels of waking consciousness, the flow of imagination, dreams, inner vision, and intuition are combined with consciousness of the spirit or sacred realms.

Based on unconditional love and service to the community, this way of being is not a form of magic or personal development that is carried out for self-benefit alone. It is a spirituality firmly rooted in the Earth, encouraging a respectful engagement with the natural world of minerals, plants, animals, landscape, and climate.

TO SUM UP

TAKING THE PATH

When you enter the space prepared for you by Maryam, you might wish to go "barefoot." Do not be afraid of being in the "dark," for you are light itself and soon to make that discovery. The farther you go along the path of the Seven Signs, the closer you will come to the sanctuary within yourself. The path is not always smooth or easy, moving as it does from the familiar to challenging landscapes that, surprisingly, sometimes shockingly, will resonate deep within you. The disruption of what you thought you knew can release the past and awaken you to what is happening right now with its provocative meanings, sounds, scents, textures, and intuitions. To undertake the journey you need to be willing to accept the unexpected and to trust that the universe in which you have put yourself will always look after you.

You are at the beginning.

7

IN THE BEGINNING

To enter into the world of Maryam's Teaching Story, we need to enter the world of the imaginal, the world of the imagination, and the world of feelings. Perhaps we have danced and sung together, then eaten a simple meal. Now we settle down in a circle to listen to Maryam. She asks us to make ourselves comfortable, to close our eyes and breathe. Then she takes us through a number of ways to relate to her, to the others in the circle, to where we are, and to the teachings. We are asked to become aware of the place where we are sitting, how we feel within ourselves, how balanced we feel. We listen to the sounds around us, the sound and scent of the air, the sounds of birds, singing or in flight. We become aware of each other, that each one of us is a divine being. We simply sit and breathe, alert and aware, yet relaxed and comfortable. Maryam speaks a prayer of thanks.

The light of the Source is within each of us, she says, reflected in the sun by day and the moon by night. The light does not fail. Maryam asks us to become aware of this light in our hearts as a feeling of love. When we are ready, we pass this light to the person on our left and imagine that it passes from person to person, joining us all together. We sit in the silence, becoming aware of the silence within us. The air seems to tremble with expectation. We are ready to hear her voice again, to see her facial expressions, her body gestures, to hear the pauses between her words as she waits for us to absorb that which she is communicating. We are ready to hear her story.

She speaks in Aramaic, her Semitic mother tongue. We need to bear this in mind, for the words we have today in the modern biblical text are a translation from the Greek, which, in turn, may well have been a translation from the Aramaic. Aramaic is a language in which each consonant has a meaning that may then become expanded when certain consonants are grouped together. For example, the name Maryam (MRYM) begins and ends with the letter *mem,* indicating water, bodies of water, and all things connected with water, including the emotional world. Her name also contains the concepts of *mar:* mastery, and *yam:* waters, while the letter *resh* indicates a ray of light and heat emanating from a central point. The inner meaning of consonants and consonant groups reflects the Semitic understanding that everything is vibrating energy. As Maryam's transformation Story unfolds, we shall see how she uses that understanding to guide her followers toward discovering the inner meaning of her teachings.

THE STORY OPENS

The Story opens with a dreamlike scene from the Palestine of two thousand years ago—the banks of the river Yarden (Jordan). There are the crowds of people, and among them, we see a shaman; weather-beaten and dressed in animal skins, he immerses people in river water to wash away their "darkness." This is Yokhanan (John). Maryam begins her story with a song and her song begins with the Aramaic word *b:* "in, at."

◆──────────────────────────────

(John 1:1–5) In the beginning was the Word, and the Word was with God, and the Word was God. He was in the beginning with God. All things came into being through him, and without him not one thing came into being. What has come into being in him was life, and the life was the light of all people. The light shines in the darkness, and the darkness did not overcome it.

Maryam pauses for a moment. "In the beginning" (*b'reshit* in Hebrew*)* happens to be the name of the first book of the Jewish Bible (Old Testament), known in English as Genesis. Her teaching will be about the creation of something new and unique.

The word *b:* "in," is written as the letter ב, having the form of a square with one open side. In the Hebrew alphabet, individual letters have meanings as well as names. This second letter of the alphabet is called *bet,* meaning "house." As we pay attention and begin to listen to Maryam, we are *in* this "house" now. Here, we stop wondering about our state of readiness to begin the journey of transformation and try to sense how we feel. We know that, somehow, our very hearts must become for us the spiritual meaning of house—the dwelling place of the soul, the holy of holies.

Maryam's listeners would know that each soul has a feminine and masculine aspect and that the feminine aspect of the soul is symbolized by the house. Look again at the sign letter for house and listen to its warm and gentle voice. It says: Even though your "house" is a sacred place, the house is open and you are free to leave at any time.

Acknowledging that her listeners have made themselves comfortable, Maryam continues. Someone is singing in Aramaic: *B'rishit etohi hwa meltah.* At first the song sounds like something from Hebrew scripture, reminiscent of the first words of the book of Genesis, but the words of the song are different. Each person in the gathering hears Maryam's story in his own way. Some hear a chant: "In the beginning was divine energy (*meltah*). This divine energy is everything . . . everything is there . . . and here. Divine energy becomes human souls. In this way, the Source becomes all of us!" To others the song is about the creation of things, but the words sound like the wisdom sayings known as the Proverbs: "In the beginning was Wisdom. She is the creative power of the Source. Wisdom becomes the stuff of life and, through her, the Holy One becomes human. This energy of Sacred Oneness becomes all of us!"

The word "beginning" moves out to every heart in the circle.

However we perceive them, the opening words of Maryam's story have the effect of reminding us, her audience, that we are at the beginning of something, something momentous—nothing less than the creation of a new person. So, at the beginning of your pilgrimage, you are taking the first steps in creating who you really are—an embodiment of sacred wisdom. And this is entirely possible because each of us is the physical form that carries the invisible, sacred reality.

Maryam pauses with a smile. Some fun will hold our attention. During the Hebrew Creation story, the Creator asks the primeval human: "Where are you?" (Genesis 3:9) as if the Creator would not already know the answer! The mystical view is that this is the primeval and eternally relevant question. As human beings we are being asked: "At this very moment, where is your heart? Where is your consciousness?" We are here on Earth, either aware or unaware. This is where Yeshua and Maryam walked and talked and loved. This is where we walk and talk and love. The way to the Mystery, and all paths to spirituality, is right here and now. The beginning is now.

LOGOS OR MELTAH

In Greek, *logos* means "word": sound energy as the manifestation or expression of the Source. Before Yeshua or any other human being was ever born into existence, this manifestation of the Source was the Source. It brought the world into being and has enlightened every creature, acting throughout the ages. That is what you can glean from the opening Greek words. But before the words of the gospel were written down, they were originally spoken in Aramaic, not Greek. Like languages such as French or Spanish, every word in Aramaic or Hebrew is either masculine or feminine. There is no neuter gender. But Maryam was well aware that the Source is not a person and is neither masculine nor feminine. From the very beginning of the gospel, she invents a poetic way, only obvious in Aramaic, of overcoming the problem of how to talk about something that has no gender in a gender-specific language. She does this by using a fascinating, almost untranslatable word to describe the sending forth of divine energies.

Thus, the Aramaic version of the gospel opens with the words of what sounds like a devotional hymn: *B'rishit etohi hwa meltah,* which translates as "In the beginning was the meltah." Here, the feminine word *meltah* is used with two masculine verb forms: *etohi* and *hwa.* Meltah, with no direct equivalent in any other language, can mean power, force, manifestation, emanation, light, substance, as well as word—and can embody all these meanings simultaneously. The consonantal structure of Aramaic words leaves them open to many meanings that are determined by the listener according to the context of the words. To Aramaic ears the first five foundational words of the gospel convey exactly what Maryam wanted to convey—that the Source cannot be defined by gender and neither can divine creative energies be summed up in a single word (which is what the Greek asks us to do). Having understood the infinite nature of what the Source is sending into manifestation, when the Greek masculine pronouns are substituted by the mystical concept of meltah, a more exciting meaning for the whole of the hymn is revealed:

(John 1:1–5) In the beginning was divine energy, and the divine energy was with God, and the divine energy was God. It was in the beginning with God. All things came into being through it, and without it not one thing came into being. What has come into being (as meltah) was life, and the life was the light of all people. The light shines in the darkness, and the darkness did not overcome it.

THE BEGINNING IS NOW: THE CONTEXT FOR THE TEACHING STORY

The Teaching Story starts with the phrase "in/at the beginning" because the beginning was not a happening in the past since the beginning is always now, we are always at the beginning. This is the vibrant message: consciousness/life/the Source is now, you are always now. We are consciousness and consciousness is each one of us.

Maryam teaches in the traditional way through carefully designed stories about Yeshua. Each story is multilayered, and so that we can understand their depths of meaning, at this beginning point she raises our consciousness. We are listening to a devotional song, and it succinctly describes Yeshua's own experience of the Source and of Creation. The song tells us that the energy of the Source—the holy breath and its sound (the "word")—was the means of creation. The realization that all life comes from the Source/God is the first step in seeing, and experiencing, all life as a manifestation of the Source. The Source is not separate from Creation—there is nothing that is not the Source. Our beginning, Maryam teaches, is this realization—the same realization that Yeshua proclaimed. It is the context in which we need to place our own perceptions of the teachings from now on.

LIGHT AND DARKNESS

A little more understanding is added at this point. "The light shines in the darkness and the darkness did not overcome it." Darkness has no judgmental or negative overtones. In a Semitic context light and dark are a continuum. Darkness is the absence of light; it cannot "overcome" light. In this sense darkness is in the process of becoming light. Always remember that. Maryam's words also reinforce her first message because they highlight again the image of the Creation story where, before there was any Creation, there was darkness—simply, the absence of light.

Darkness has a further layer of meaning. Maryam is talking about the opposite of *gnosis*—ignorance or the state of not having inner knowing. This is why she paused for us to ask ourselves where we are, where is our consciousness? It does not matter at this early stage if we are not sure. It does not matter if we have not yet experienced inner knowing, for we will be helped to reach that awareness within our Heart Space. The light shines in the darkness. Don't worry, be happy!

JOHN THE IMMERSER

With this understanding the story switches to the role of John the Immerser and why he is featured in the story. Perhaps he was the one singing Maryam's opening song.

(John 1: 6-9) There was a man sent from God, whose name was John. He came as a witness to testify to the light, so that all might believe through him. He himself was not the light, but he came to testify to the light. The true light, which enlightens everyone, was coming into the world.

John the Immerser was "a man sent from God"—a shaman—who was living in the deserts around Jerusalem. Clothed in camel skins, secured with a leather girdle around his waist, the figure of John the Immerser would have resonated with Maryam's followers, recalling the ancestral beings Adam and Khava (Eve) who dressed in "garments of skins" (Genesis 3:21). He dramatically represents the first human beings who were at the beginning, after the emergence of Light. He spoke to the people about the divine light that was available to all, not just a few priests or educated men. In the redaction of this first chapter, John's teaching about the divine light morphs into a description of a human being who embodies the qualities of meltah: Yeshua (Jesus).

(John 1:10–11) He (the true light) was in the world, and the world came into being through him (the true light); yet the world did not know him (the true light). He came to what was his own, and his own people did not accept him.

John is the symbol that the people have been prepared for a leap in human evolution and an expansion of consciousness. But when Yeshua appears he is only recognized by those whose inner eyes have been opened. The soul called Yeshua comes into a body, bringing a great message from the Holy One. When each one of us is born, all people tend to see is a beautiful baby; few realize who it is that has just arrived on the planet—a divine soul. This also seems to be the case with Yeshua, John says, for even though they live close to this person, very few people are aware of whom he might be. Yeshua will have to do something to awaken the people to the truth of who they really are. For those whose inner eyes have been opened, he may become their teacher. This is why they called him Rabbi.

(John 1:12–13) But to all who received him, who believed in his name, he gave power to become children of God, who were born, not of blood or of the will of the flesh or of the will of man, but of God.

WHAT NAMES REALLY MEAN

In the Semitic tradition, all possible meanings may be present in the words of a shaman-prophet or the words of a sacred scripture. This encourages the listener and the reader to perceive any statement in more than one way and to explore what they are hearing and listen for what resonates for them. The consonantal structure of Aramaic and Hebrew words presents opportunities for a rich and poetic play on words, rhyme, and repetition of sounds. The insertion of vowels further increases the possibilities for multiple translations and interpretations of any statement. But the redactor's approach to the text of the Gospel of John insists on a single meaning, in Greek, that aligns with Christian dogma. Aramaic scholars, such as Neil Douglas-Klotz, feel that because of this approach, modern readers of the Bible, translated as it is from biblical

Greek, miss out on important subtle meanings as well as the humor and poetry of Aramaic wordplay.

A good example is the word *shemah,* a word that has much more to convey than its translation: "name," since the consonants ShM indicate atmosphere, vibration, light, even an energetic field or aura, all in a process of expansion. Think about your name, or the name that you are known by. Do you like your name? Some people feel uncomfortable with their given name and change it. In many indigenous cultures, people are given different names to signify changes in maturity and experience. Your name is a word, but a very special word because it carries your vibration and your light.

The Semitic concept is that every name carries a particular energy within the sound of its consonants and vowels. In the middle of Yeshua's name is the magical letter ש *shin:* eternal flame, representing the holy spirit/breath and the flame of divine revelation. Like holy men and women of the time, Yeshua had a powerful energy field that not only supported those who sought to expand their consciousness, but actually accelerated their progress. With this understanding, we can see that verse 12 above is also talking about those who choose to immerse themselves in the vibration of Yeshua—a more profound action than mere belief.

In the same tradition, because it vibrates, it resonates. Everything is resonating. We pick up some of the resonation around us as sound. We also sense subtle forms of resonation, such as the atmosphere in a room or building, or the feelings that another person is emanating. The Gospel of Signs begins with a reference to sound deliberately because it alerts us to the power and significance of the oral teachings of both Yeshua and Maryam. The oral teachings of transformation take the listener back to the beginning of Creation and the beginning of resonation. This is where we must put ourselves—at the time our soul chose to incarnate as a human being, when divine energy became flesh.

(John 1:14) And the Word became flesh and lived among us, and we have seen his glory, the glory as of a father's only son, full of grace and truth.

The phrase "he lived," or "dwelt among us," is rendered in Aramaic as "pitched his tent," a phrase that would help the listener recall the times of living in the desert, the times of shamanic wisdom. All the great Hebrew teachers were shamans, for Holy Wisdom made her home in such persons. We can tell that because they exhibit the qualities of charisma, direct communication with the spirit world and the Source, prophecy, healing, and teaching, qualities that are present in any person who has a close alignment with the sacred. Even when the Hebrews began to settle in towns and villages, they still used many shamanic practices, such as working with certain plants and trees and burning incense, but they referred to them less and less. Male priests took over the role of spiritual guardians and gave the people dogma, prescribed ritual and literal interpretation of the written word—roles that gave them secular as well as religious power.

He "pitched his tent among us" also means that he came to live among Maryam's people, in the Galilee. The divine energy, which is in all of us, becomes a particular human being who, embodying the qualities of meltah, actually emanates the divine energy. This is perceived by some as glowing light, especially around the head. This is the "glory" so often mentioned, which is present throughout the cosmos as an emanation that can be perceived by the shaman. John sees the radiance around Yeshua and notes that no one realizes who Yeshua might be. He walks and Maryam knows that walk.

JOHN'S TESTIMONY

In the modern text, John's song ends abruptly, leaving us to wonder whether something has been left out or significantly changed. As if another voice is speaking, we now hear of his encounter with the Temple authorities, in a testimony that is obviously designed to tell the listener/reader a little more about the dazzling person whom he has not yet named—yet, if you believe in his name, great things are promised. John was obviously talking about the power of this person's energy field or vibration.

◆———————————————————————————

(John 1:19–28) This is the testimony given by John when the Jews sent priests and Levites from Jerusalem to ask him, "Who are you?" He confessed, "I am not the Messiah." And they asked him, "What then? Are you Elijah?" He said, "I am not." "Are you the prophet?" He answered, "No." Then they said to him, "Who are you? Let us have an answer for those who sent us. What do you say about yourself?" He said, "I am the voice of one crying out in the wilderness, 'Make straight the way of the Lord,' as the prophet Isaiah said." Now they had been sent from the Pharisees. They asked him, "Why then are you baptizing if you are neither the Messiah, nor Elijah, nor the prophet?" John answered them, "I baptize with water. Among you stands one whom you do not know, the one who is coming after me; I am not worthy to untie the thong of his sandal." This took place in Bethany across the Jordan where John was baptizing.

The "Jews," as they appear in biblical accounts, were originally the people of Yehudah (Judea), as opposed to Galileans, such as John, Yeshua, and Maryam. John's shamanic work of immersion in the River Jordan had caused a stir that got back to the authorities in Jerusalem. They dispatched officials to investigate what was going on. Interestingly, the ensuing conversation shows that it was accepted at the time that men and women could be the incarnation of holy people from the past; but the identity of "the prophet" is not yet mentioned. John's quote from the words of Isaiah would have alerted listeners of the time to the implications of the statement, especially the word "wilderness," which becomes a recurring theme throughout Maryam's transformational teachings. Isaiah too was a shaman-prophet whose task was to prepare the people by raising their awareness to divine presence. Remember, in Semitic time, in Maryam's Story time, the past is also now.

On the political front, there are people close to the Roman puppet governor, Herod, who want to be rid of John. But still he seems relaxed and smiling, as if he doesn't know about the danger or perhaps could not have cared less. This later adaptation of John's encounter with religious and Temple officials still offers intriguing and useful depths for the pilgrim traveler. Listeners of the time were put directly in touch with their Hebrew tradition with the mention of the shaman-prophet Eliyahu (Elijah) and the direct quote from the words of the shaman-prophet Yeshayah (Isaiah 40:3). So this tells us that the as-yet-unnamed person is another great shaman-prophet and we are being psychologically and spiritually prepared for an encounter with this person.

Then, almost as an afterthought, or aside, we are told that the opening scene to Maryam's Teaching Story is taking place near a village named Bethany. But we know that the mention of any place, like the mention of any person, is significant. We now have a place name for the beginning of our journey: Bet Anyah ("House of the Poor"). Bethany lies a few miles east of the temple city of Yerushalayim (Jerusalem).

WHO IS THE NEW SHAMAN-PROPHET?

John says that he did not know the new shaman-prophet—and we have still not been given his name—but he knew that he had to prepare the people for the energetic presence of the new prophet by immersing them in "living" water.

(John 1:31) I did not know him; but I came baptizing with water
for this reason, that he might be revealed to Israel.

From now on the Story continues to refer to water, embodied as it is
in Maryam's name and in her very teaching presence. In the Semitic
worldview, light is most potent when it radiates, and it is then compared
to the flow of water. Thus references to water simultaneously evoke references to spiritual light, and the movement of water to the radiation of
spiritual light.

(John 1:32–33) And John testified, "I saw the Spirit descending
from heaven like a dove, and it remained on him. I myself did not
know him, but the one who sent me to baptize with water said to
me, 'He on whom you see the Spirit descend and remain is the one
who baptizes with the Holy Spirit.'"

The day after his encounter with the Jerusalem officials, John uses
the traditional Semitic symbol of a descending white dove to tell people
how he has seen the light of Yeshua's spiritual energy emanating around
Yeshua's head. This was the sign confirming that Yeshua was the holy
man for whom he had been waiting. In case there is any doubt, John turns
to us (as listeners to the story), shaking his shaggy head and repeating that
he did not know the new shaman-prophet. This man is definitely not
one of his followers. But John intuits that while he can immerse people
in living water, to cleanse them, this is simply part of his role as preparer.
Yeshua is empowered to go further, to immerse them in the holy breath,
to breathe the creative spirit into a person. He can awaken them directly.

I have often pondered over who was there to witness the important conversations between John and the Jerusalem officials, as well
as all the other conversations in the Gospel of Signs. In fact we may
find ourselves wondering about the identity of the witness throughout

Maryam's Story. On reflection, since it is her story, she is the most likely witness. Much more significant is the convention of the Story—we have to look behind the words and listen to what the story is telling us. This is the teaching of the fourth level of understanding.

YOU ARE AT THE CREATION

Maryam tells us that from the outset we are at the beginning. We are born with the power to create our life. Your life is your creation story. The biblical Creation story is a graphic, mythical record of the principles of the cosmos, which underlie the ongoing creative processes of life, according to traditional wisdom that the Creation story is not about events that happened in some distant past time, but in what indigenous Australians call "the Dreaming" or "Dreamtime." "Days" in the Creation story are seven pulses of illumination and darkness, knowing and unknowing, expansion and contraction, and this energetic movement continues into the present. In other words Creation is always happening now.

This is made clear in the picture of the seven-day week. The Creation—within Dreamtime—took place over six "days," culminating in the seventh day, which is the Sabbath. This is dream language for the place to which human beings are journeying. The Sabbath is the heaven state. This day is now dedicated to experiencing the heaven state in as many ways as possible because it is the day of remembrance of who we really are. In this way eternal reality is periodically manifested in the cycle of the week. The Seven Signs relate to this cosmic creative week. The sign relating to the Sabbath is that one where realization of spiritual reality is total—the Seventh Sign, relating to resurrection and rebirth. The Seventh Sign is the outcome of recovering sacred, or shamanic, vision in the Sixth Sign where we can at last "see" where the interior and exterior cosmic week is leading. In a sense the Sabbath is also a spiritual *place:* the heart center.

All this beauty and movement is conjured up by the opening words of Maryam's story. She is also saying that, just as Genesis is the start of the Torah—the five books of Moses—her teaching is like another Torah. She will underline this image with allusions to many of the great biblical figures such as Moses, Jacob, Joshua, David, Elijah, Elisha, and Joseph the dream interpreter. In an ingenious twist to her story, Maryam finally brings us back to the beginning by returning Yeshua and his followers to Bethany. This tells us that her Teaching Story may have begun a Torah, but our own transformational journey in following the Seven Signs completes it. Day 1 (Sign 1), Day 2 (Sign 2), Day 3 (Sign 3), Day 4 (Sign 4), Day 5 (Sign 5), Day 6 (Sign 6), Day 7: Shabbat (Sign 7). The procession of the Signs and days of the week is truly cyclic, for, after we reach the Seventh Sign of resurrection and rebirth, we will see that we have been reunited with Sign One. We are literally reunited with the Source.

From the very beginning of our journey of transformation, Maryam is asking us to bear in mind that the character, words, and actions of Yeshua are an allegory. In her Teaching Story, Yeshua symbolizes your sacred soul—the one who recognizes and celebrates the integration of heaven and Earth, the spiritual and the physical, and the eternal unity of the Source with each individual person.

A SIGN OF CHANGES TO COME

Maryam's followers would have known exactly who John the Immerser was, and they would have understood the importance of his ritual immersions. But they would also know that his place in the transformation story is deliberate and points to a meaning they must discover for themselves. Some of this meaning can be found in the restorative words of one of the great shaman-prophets, Yekhezk'el (Ezekiel), as they have been recorded: "Thus says the Lord God . . . I will sprinkle clean water upon you . . . I will cleanse you. A new heart I will give to you, and a new spirit I will put within you; and I will remove from your body the heart of stone and give you a heart of flesh." (Ezekiel 36:25–26). This man of visions, who lived through the destruction of the Jerusalem Temple by the Babylonians, was determined to present a vision of hope to the people.

John also presents a vision of hope to the officials sent from Jerusalem. There is little in the existing text to tell us whether they understood that he was simply preparing people for an inner realization. This realization will occur, says John, when the unnamed shaman-prophet immerses a person in the energies of the Holy Spirit. In Aramaic, *rukhah:* spirit, breath, wind, air, implies the emanation in all directions (R) of the life force (Kh). This sacred breath is what animated the primordial human and continues to animate all living beings. Yeshua can awaken people to their innate divine nature by energizing the life force within them by literally immersing them in the atmosphere or vibration of the sacred breath. Thus, they will not have to journey to a river or place of "living waters" for this to happen. We will come across this form of awakening in each of the Seven Signs that follow.

People at that time assumed that the messiah was someone who would lead, overcome enemies, save, and redeem. But Yeshua taught that we all have a messiah and a teacher within us—our soul. Our soul is the anointed one (khristos in Greek), not some exalted person. We are not told whether John the Immerser had this insight, though, being a shaman, we can assume that he did. But Maryam's point is that from the beginning, realizing that we are spiritual beings means listening to the voice of the "inner messiah." From now on we will need to listen carefully to the voice of our own hearts.

Maryam's followers also realize that the appearance of Yeshua and Maryam marks a radical new psychological and spiritual maturity in the development of the relationship between the Hebrews (as representatives of all human beings) and the Source. This had been predicted by other shaman-prophets, such as Yirmeyahu (Jeremiah 31:33–34), for example. The breakthrough comes centuries later with the figure of John who leaves his village home and sets off into the wilderness.

Here, he discovers his mission to act out the words of Ezekiel and so prepare human beings for the presence, and energies, of Yeshua and Maryam.

In the desert wilderness, inner resources are put to the test, for there is no established path to follow, and no security, and a person soon finds out if his inner resources are soul-based. It is here, in the desert wilderness, not far from the symbolic village of Bethany, that John realizes that a break with the spirituality of the past is imminent. He discovers that relationship with the Divine has to move from fear to love and that this new relationship would tell anyone that certain practices were now unnecessary. All ritual, including hymns, psalms, prayer, and dance, can celebrate our oneness with All That Is, but the sacrifice of animals, for example, is part of a primitive past.

TO SUM UP

MARYAM'S BEGINNING CHALLENGE

In very ancient times, when the Australian Aborigines looked into the wilderness, what was then wild Australia, they felt the presence of Sacred Creation within the Earth and within the cosmos, not outside, somewhere else. This understanding meant that everything was sacred—the landscape, every animal (including humans), every plant, no matter how small or seemingly insignificant. That indigenous, shamanic worldview continues intact to this day, and it is exactly what is described in the very first verse of the Gospel of Signs. In the Beginning there is the energy of the Sacred and that energy *is* the Sacred. There is nothing that is not the Source.

Here we have Maryam's twofold challenge. From the first moment that you take up the path of the Seven Signs, you will need to understand that you are at the beginning of your life today and that everything is sacred, without exceptions. You will then need to experience these two understandings as feelings. To make these discoveries for yourself, you may well need to spend some time in the "wilderness."

8

WALKING IN THE WILDERNESS, DISCOVERING THE I AM

Before we set out on our pilgrimage, Maryam asks us to pay attention to how the Story begins and how it ends and where the Story begins and where it ends. Being a pilgrim is being a wanderer in a sacred land. The chant that sings of our new beginning places us in a virtual landscape—to the east of Jerusalem, in the wilderness that flanked Israel's eastern border. On the surface the Signs stories describe the wanderings of a band of pilgrims from the village of Bethany, north to their birthplace in the Galilee, and finally back to Bethany.

Situated near the wilderness, Bethany was separated from Jerusalem by the Kidron Valley, whose sides, since ancient times, were used for rock-hewn tombs. Recent archaeology in the area around Bethany has revealed a great many ossuaries bearing the names of Galileans. It seems highly probable that being near the end of a well-used pilgrim route, Bethany was settled by Galileans. Maryam's listeners would have known this. We may well be within sight of Jerusalem in Judea, the home of religious orthodoxy, but are we actually going to be immersed in the revolutionary spirituality of the Galilee—a spirituality directly descended from the shamanic, wilderness origins of Judaism? We will soon find out.

WILDERNESS ORIGINS

Wilderness, or wild land, is still defined as a natural environment that has not been significantly modified by human activity, a wild place that humans do not control and have not developed in any way. Today wilderness is deeply valued for cultural, spiritual, and aesthetic reasons. Some nature writers, such as Daniel Botkin, believe that wilderness areas are vital for the human spirit and for creativity. The town or city dweller still needs the magic and challenge of wildness. Thoreau saw wildness as a state of mind and was convinced that "in wildness is the preservation of the world."

The natural world tells us that "wild" is how life really is. Wild is not antagonistic and wilderness is not a place to be feared. Wild simply has to be respected and its own divine nature acknowledged.

It took many years of traveling back and forth across the same wilderness for the Israelites to cleanse themselves of generations of slavery and become free on every level. It took this time for them to take responsibility for their own destiny, to believe in themselves, and to dream again. Wandering in any kind of wilderness is often the initiation rite for becoming a complete human being, for the wilderness initiation is the journey toward the soul. In *The Hirsch Haggadah,* the nineteenth-century rabbi Samson Hirsch wrote that the Israelites were led into the wilderness so that they could deal with their anxiety. Anxiety, Hirsch suggests, is the real slavery—a condition that we perpetuate within ourselves by not taking responsibility for our lives. Anxiety follows when we depend on others for our sense of self and when we blame others for the situations in which we find ourselves. But time in the wilderness, says Hirsch, can help us reclaim our sacred self.

Whatever our background, our distant ancestors were wilderness dwellers. Wilderness is part of our genetic code. Human beings found that the wilderness is a great test of whether a community is sustainable. For the Hebrew travelers, the system of law developed to deal with the concerns of a tribal, nomadic, wilderness community, was called *halakhah,* derived from the root HLKh, "to walk." The system was designed to teach the art of "walking," in every sense. The experience of wilderness helps us to find out who we are, and we learn how to live in community with other people. In the process we have the opportunity to see our particular form of slavery for what it is, to purify ourselves, to receive visions, to forge closer contacts with the spirit world, to develop intimacy with other people and the land over which we wander. It is no coincidence, then, that Maryam gathers her followers in the wilderness where they will begin their pilgrimage. Today, we, too, must join this band in this imaginal place.

The Teaching Story may be taken as it is, just a story about people and places, their dreams and aspirations, their mistakes and disappointments; but if we have decided to make the pilgrimage to reclaim our sacred self, the inner magical us, then the Story reveals other dimensions that make it universal and relevant, regardless of time, place, and culture.

WALKING TO THE THREE FESTIVALS

From the soul's point of view, we do not have any real identity until we find ourselves, but traditionally a spiritual journey offers a way to self-discovery.

The Jewish seasonal celebrations provide the opportunity to integrate time in the wilderness into daily life at least three times a year, via the regular pilgrimage festivals of Pesakh, Shavuot, and Sukkot. These harvest festivals were times when people traveled long distances from all over Israel and beyond to bring offerings to the Temple in Jerusalem. The three festivals were collectively called the *shalosh regalim,* the "three on foot" days. As we shall see, Maryam deliberately includes this festival period to highlight the message that pilgrimage, going on foot, feeling the ground beneath our feet, and taking in our surroundings, is an essential part of the transformation story. You learn how to be a pilgrim by becoming one.

A PLACE OF RESONATION

Tribal people have never regarded wilderness as a threat. Rather, it is a place to befriend, where one can discover both the mystery of creation and oneself. The ancient Hebrew word for wilderness, the scene of so much transformation and new beginnings, is *midbar*, "that which resonates." In the rugged expanse of wilderness, wildness resonates as spiritual communication, the call of the soul, the call of the sacred world of Nature—the unveiled face of the Source. The call of the wild says that the mystery is inside you, was inside you all the time, you just needed to be somewhere where the call could resonate, where the voice of your soul could be heard. This happens when you enter into the deep silence within, either out in Nature or in the depths of your heart.

LIBERATION:
DISCOVERING THE I AM

While still at the beginning of Maryam's Teaching Story, before we discover the identity of "the prophet," references to the area around Bethany tell us that we have not yet left the wilderness, the place of resonation. One of the challenges that wilderness presents is the question of identity. As you look at your surroundings, you cannot help identifying things by their name. Wilderness then responds with the unexpected: "Do the names you give to things help describe what is happening to you as you experience them?" Wilderness may even ask whether your name is who you are or even describes who you are. For ancient Semitic people, and indigenous people of today, name embodies the atmosphere and vibration, the very resonation, of a person, animal, place, or thing. Now Maryam deliberately uses "name" in this context to awaken her followers (and so us) to a specific moment in their ancestral history.

Many centuries before the wilderness had gifted the world with a great treasure. According to the story in Exodus, the experience of the

Hebrew people had prepared them for a more advanced concept of the Holy One. In the past the people knew "him" as the Almighty, a power far greater than anything they could imagine. They had been liberated from the bondage of slavery; now they were ready to be liberated from the bondage of ignorance. They were ready to learn the deeper truth of the Godsource.

The story tells how, after leading the Hebrew people away from Egypt and into the desert wilderness, the shaman-prophet Moses took time out to rest on a rocky hilltop. In his exhausted state, as he sees a burning bush that remains unconsumed by fire, he experiences a profound vision of what it is to be divine. Should he tell the people, and, if so, how should he do this? How to name such a revelation? In answer to his questions, the Holy One says enigmatically: *"Ehyeh asher ehyeh."* In Hebrew this means "I am what I am" and simultaneously "I will be what I will be." In time these words were encapsulated in the "name" I AM. In effect the I AM had said to Moses: "I am the unlimited and indescribable Being that manifests throughout the reality of which you, and they, are aware. I am all that you see, all that you know, all that you sense. I am in the heart of each of you, and of each facet and part of Creation." This would not have thrown Moses, for he had experienced the Godsource as an ongoing, living process rather than a superhuman patriarchal figure. Nevertheless, he might have been overwhelmed with this new understanding as, suddenly, the culmination of his life's mission was revealed. He has been sent to help his people, and all people, realize that I AM is their true self.

The history of Jewish spirituality shows that I AM is celebrated in Hebrew as "Anokhi" and in Aramaic as "Ena-ena," but the implications of the name—that the I AM is present in the heart of every person—remained the understanding of mystics alone. This understanding comes directly from the realization that everything is a manifestation of the Holy One. It was the central teaching of the mystic Yeshua, as we shall see in his use of the name I AM, a teaching that enraged those religious authorities who insisted on the separation between a person, the Creation, and the Godsource. This is still the situation in our own time where religious authorities thrive on our sense of separation from our divine self, and the divine presence within all that is.

By reminding us of an extraordinary wilderness event, Maryam bolsters Yeshua's experience of the sacred and urges us to remember who we really are: the I AM, temporarily residing within the named person we consider ourselves to be. It cannot be otherwise, for I AM is all that is.

TO SUM UP

"WILDERNESS" IS A WAY OF BEING

When you enter into the silence of the heart—as in deep meditation, or the heightened states of consciousness demanded by a healing session or ceremony—you find yourself in the wilderness, the place of resonation. The wilderness is the best place to prepare for transformation. There, too much baggage is a weight you can do without. Too much of anything is a distraction. In the wilderness the watchword is "keep it simple." Wilderness, then, is a way of being, and with the determination to walk in this way, we will, sooner or later, raise our consciousness to become aware of the I AM within us. Now we are ready to set off northward, from the Jordan valley to the green tracks of the Galilee and the first of Maryam's Signs. But before that, having discovered who we really are, some introductions to our traveling companions are in order, especially the identity of "the prophet."

9

THE PROPHET
AND
THE ANGELS

The Gospel of John (1:35–36) continues,

> The next day John again was standing with two of his disciples,
> and as he watched Jesus walk by, he exclaimed, "Look, here is the
> Lamb of God!"

John is back on the river bank doing the ritual cleansing he always does.
People are chatting. He must have performed some powerful healings,
for some wonder if he is an incarnation of the prophet Eliyahu (Elijah).
Suddenly, Yeshua passes by. We have at last been given his name. But
who are the *two* disciples of John? One of them bears the Greek name
Andreas (Andrew). The other is Maryam, the nameless witness. The
title "Lamb of God" was obviously added by a later redactor to fit
with Christian ideas about Jesus as sacrificial "lamb," a title that might
have been confusing to listeners at the time because sheep *follow* the
shepherd.

THE MOMENTOUS MEETING

(John 1:37–40) The two disciples heard him say this, and they followed Jesus. When Jesus turned and saw them following, he said to them, "What are you looking for?" They said to him, "Rabbi" (which translated means Teacher), "where are you staying?" He said to them, "Come and see." They came and saw where he was staying, and they remained with him that day. It was about four o'clock in the afternoon. One of the two who heard John speak and followed him was Andrew, Simon Peter's brother.

Maryam (the unnamed follower) and Andrew decide to test out John's description of the new teacher. They pick up their travel bags and follow Yeshua. He stops, turns round, and looks them straight in the eyes. This is the momentous meeting where Yeshua recognizes Maryam and she recognizes him. The energies of this first encounter have not only endured to our time, but have actually gained momentum.

"What are you looking for?" asks Yeshua, knowing exactly what they are looking for. In reply both of John's followers ask: "Teacher, where are you staying?" Yeshua laughs and invites them to "come and see." This traditional Semitic way to approach a teacher is still common in contemporary indigenous cultures. They follow him to his tent where they can no longer hear the river, or the people, or the thundering voice of John. They sit down and Yeshua gives them water and some bread and dates. They spend the rest of the day together. Yeshua would have spoken to them as if he knew the contents of each of their hearts and minds.

Andreas is the third figure with a message for the pilgrim traveler. His name in Greek means brave. For the listener the symbolism is that those who follow the Rabbi, and now those who follow Maryam, will need to be brave and courageous. Andrew stands next to her. This image shows us that she has those qualities, and with hindsight, we know that she is going to need them. Further, those who follow the voice of the soul will need to be brave and courageous too.

THE MEET-UP WITH ROCKY

In a redaction based on hindsight, we have been told in advance that Andreas has a brother, Shimon, who will soon be known to Christians by his Greek-based name Peter.

(John 1:41–42) He first found his brother Simon and said to him, "We have found the Messiah" (which is translated Anointed). He brought Simon to Jesus, who looked at him and said, "You are Simon son of John. You are to be called Cephas" (which is translated Peter).

The landscape changes again. Andrew says he must go and get his brother Shimon to meet Yeshua. We are left thinking how strange that one brother is Greek (a Hebrew family would not then have given a male child a Greek name unless they had already embraced Hellenistic culture), and the other is Hebrew, but this is Maryam's deliberate intent to show that people of different nations are in fact "brothers." Shimon arrives and Yeshua looks at him, assessing his nature. He laughs when he hears that Shimon's nickname is Rocky. So he is known in Aramaic as Shimon Kefa. In Greek the joke goes further because Shimon's nickname sounds very like the Greek word *kefali,* "head." So perhaps this Shimon has a head like a rock? Other texts of the time, such as the Gospel of Mary show that he is indeed stubborn as well as intolerant, especially when it comes to accepting the very presence of a woman, let alone her teachings. The modern translation from the Greek carefully avoids this fun by calling him

Simon Peter, from *petros,* "rock." We know that by the time her story comes to be told, Maryam has encountered fear and enmity in the person of Simon Peter. He is not alone in being like that, but she knows that he, too, is a soul.

In spite of Rocky's well-recorded misogyny, Maryam brings him into the story for very pertinent reasons. Just as in dreams, all characters mentioned are significant because they have something to tell us about ourselves through what they say and what they do. One of our own qualities may be the strength, and even the hardness, of stone. Or does that stone speak of stubbornness or difficulty with change? If we feel this within us, we will have to decide how we use these qualities. There may be rocky times ahead!

ANGELS ASCENDING AND DESCENDING

(John 1:43–51) The next day Jesus decided to go to Galilee. He found Philip and said to him, "Follow me." Now Philip was from Bethsaida, the city of Andrew and Peter. Philip found Nathanael and said to him, "We have found him about whom Moses in the law and also the prophets wrote, Jesus son of Joseph from Nazareth." Nathanael said to him, "Can anything good come out of Nazareth?" Philip said to him, "Come and see." When Jesus saw Nathanael coming toward him, he said of him, "Here is truly an Israelite in whom there is no deceit!" Nathanael asked him, "Where did you get to know me?" Jesus answered, "I saw you under the fig tree before Philip called you." Nathanael replied, "Rabbi, you are the Son of God! You are the King of Israel!" Jesus answered, "Do you believe because I told you that I saw you under the fig tree? You will see greater things than these." And he said to him, "Very truly, I tell you, you will see heaven opened and the angels of God ascending and descending upon the Son of Man."

Another change of scene shows us that the river and John have disappeared. Yeshua, the nomadic teacher, decides to leave Judea and take his followers on a long trek to the northern shore of Lake Kinneret (Sea of Galilee) bordering the country known as the Galilee of the Goyim, a part of the Galilee that had originally been settled by foreigners, taken there by their Assyrian captors. From these immigrants the characteristic Galilean accent of later times spread throughout the region. Perhaps Maryam wants to signal that our pilgrimage has now begun with a movement away from the starting point of Bethany. She gives us another clue about Yeshua's choice of direction with her mention of the fishing town of Bet Tzaidah (Bethsaida: "House of Fishing"). In a symbolic sense he is going fishing. This, we are told, is the hometown of Andreas, Shimon Kefa (Peter) and a new character whom Yeshua seeks out, Filippos, the Greek scribe who later creates his own gospel (the Gospel of Philip). As a close follower of Maryam, and privy to her work, he may well have been the first to make a written account of her teachings.

Though he had the shamanic gift of prophecy, there is no mention in the Old Testament of Moses making prophetic writings about a Yeshua Ben-Yosef from Nazareth. Since most authorities doubt whether Moses could read or write, the passage about "Moses and the law" looks like a later pious reworking of a reference used by Judean stand-up comics about hillbillies from the north. However, we are about to find out that Yeshua is no ordinary country dweller. Just as in a dream, Philip is suddenly in another place talking to a Hebrew called Natan'el (Nathanael) who sits in the shade of a fig tree, half asleep. "We have found this wonderful rabbi from Nazareth," says Philip. "He speaks like a prophet." Nathanael makes a face and scoffs—after all the whole country is full of prophets. "Can anything good come out of that dreary little town?" "All right, come and see for yourself," says Philip. Reluctantly Nathanael gets up and follows him. Yeshua sees them approaching. "Well, well," he says, "here's an Israelite. Perhaps he can recognize truth when he comes across it." Nathanael says aggressively: "What do you mean, Israelite?

Who are you? I don't know you so how do you know anything about me?" Yeshua just smiles. "Before Philip called out to you, I saw you sitting in the shade of a fig tree." Nathanael is startled and realizes Yeshua must be a seer. Recovering quickly he says: "So you are the prophet they're all talking about." Yeshua laughs at his gullibility. "Do you believe I'm a prophet simply because I told you I saw you under the fig tree?" Nathanael feels stupid, but Yeshua turns to the followers standing there. "One day you'll see greater things than second sight. When your eyes are really open, you'll see heavenly messengers coming down to commune with this human being and going back up to heaven, and this human being is just like yourselves." Yeshua looks at them, into their hearts. Then he says gently: "And do not believe anything until you have tested it for yourselves. Whether it is written down or spoken by some learned person or someone who seemingly works wonders or even someone with second sight." He smiles at this and they all laugh.

JACOB THE GOD-WRESTLER

The Hebrew listener would have immediately made a link between Yeshua's words and the scriptural story of the patriarch Ya'akov (Jacob). During Jacob's adventurous life, he is said to have wrestled with the angels of El (God). Like most of us, he wrestled with the whole concept of the Godsource and spiritual reality—he was a God-wrestler, an Israelite. That may be why we are on this pilgrimage—we too are wrestling with the whole idea of spirituality. Maryam knows this. It's okay to be a God-wrestler. But as we ponder on this, we find that Maryam has prepared us for a second, more profound understanding that emerges from Jacob's adventures.

Jacob was on a long journey to find a wife in some distant place and stopped in the desert for the night, laying down with a cloth over a smooth stone for a pillow. He dreams that a light stretches from the ground up to heaven. Divine messengers (angels) are going up and down the light as if it is a ladder. According to the scripture, the message from the Source is that Jacob and his people, the Israelites, will be given land that they will keep forever. Jacob wakes from the dream and realizes that the Holy One must have been close at hand and he did not know it. He is angry with himself. To atone for his ignorance, and to mark the spot, he sets the stone pillow in the ground and pours a libation of oil on it, naming it Bet El (Bethel: "House of the Holy One").

Maryam alerts us to the fact that Yeshua has come to awaken the people to their own divine reality. In the Teaching Story, she takes us to her own country, the Galilee, where she was born and grew up. This is also Yeshua's country. We are warned not to make hasty judgments about place and where people come from. At the same time, the echo of the Jacob story reminds us that any, and every, place in which we find ourselves is sacred.

NATHANAEL THE SKEPTIC

Maryam's friend and assistant, Philip, has recognized Yeshua as a special prophet and wants others to do the same. He will talk to anyone who will listen about the Rabbi's teachings and goes to find a known skeptic (Nathanael). We find Nathanael sitting out of the sun in the shade of a fig tree. Perhaps this means that he does not enjoy the light of the Rabbi's teachings. The skeptic scoffs at the idea of a prophet coming from a little backwater like Nazareth. Nathanael may be without guile, but to survive in those times, he bends with the wind. Does he even recognize truth when it hits him between the eyes?

Yeshua warns this skeptic, and so warns all who hear his voice, that abilities, such as those of seers, are not necessarily signs of spiritual excellence. A prophet is not a fortune-teller, nor an experienced medium. A prophet tells you how things really are, which may not be how you think they are. Knowing this people should look for one who guides them to experience of the Holy One. The Jacob story continues the lesson, saying that the teacher will assure the people that the very ground is part of the Holy One, the place where they stand is sacred, not the temples alone. Like Yeshua, Maryam knows that her followers will identify with the image of the dreamer because they are familiar with the story of the House of El.

THE MESSENGERS

Finally, the image of the messengers occurs in both Jacob's dream and our dream story. The picture of a special dream within a dreamlike story is a good omen for us. We have an echo of the first dream, which began at the beginning. It is helpful, at this point, to think of the flow of divine energy as actual beings. Children are taught that heaven—the realm of spirit—is up there, where the great birds fly high. It is not surprising then that the image of the heavenly messenger (*angelos* in Greek) is that of a winged being. Yeshua points out that the Divine is constantly sending these "messengers" to us here on the Earth. At the same time, a record of what an individual is experiencing goes back to the One Source, as if conveyed by a messenger. The cycle of life is sacred and eternal. In the dream story, Yeshua is hinting that he will make these happenings understandable as well as visible to his followers. They are understandable and visible to Maryam and she makes such things clear to her followers through the progress of her Teaching Story. But interestingly, none of the canonical gospels have Jesus teaching about divine energy or the purpose of souls. We have to go to the Gnostic texts to find anything like that. So we have to wonder: Are some of Yeshua's teachings missing from the canon? If so, were they ever there or were they erased? Unless, of course, we listen to Maryam's opening words with Aramaic ears. Yeshua/Jesus and Maryam/Mary Magdalene were messengers who proclaimed the reality of I AM and the heart-centered way to reveal and express the I AM within.

TO SUM UP

GET READY TO SENSE THE ENERGIES
OF TRANSFORMATION

From the start mention of angelic messengers points out the transformational movement of energy that will be taking place once you begin
to work with Maryam's teachings. Yeshua's words say something like:
"You ain't seen nothing yet," which will turn out to be exactly true.
As you progress you will become aware of the energetic transactions
between the physical and spiritual levels of being. Now, with the first
set of introductions over, we are ready to travel, to encounter the first
of the Signs.

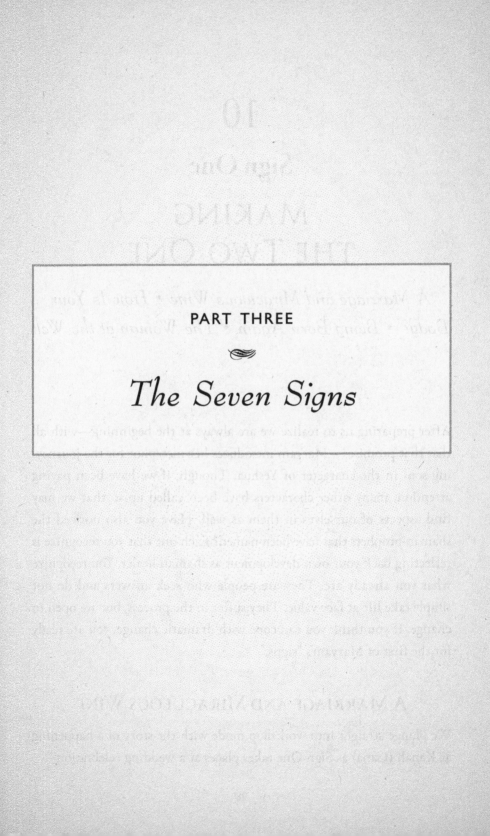

PART THREE

❧

The Seven Signs

10

Sign One

MAKING
THE TWO ONE

*A Marriage and Miraculous Wine • How Is Your
Body? • Being Born Again • The Woman at the Well*

After preparing us to realize we are always at the beginning—with all
that that promises—Maryam introduces her metaphor for the journeying soul in the character of Yeshua. Though, if we have been paying
attention, many other characters have been called up so that we may
find aspects of ourselves in them as well. Have you also noticed the
shaman-prophets that have been named? Each one that you recognize is
reflecting back your own development as shaman-healer. You recognize
what you already are. They are people who seek answers and do not
simply take life at face value. They suffer in the process, but are open to
change. If you think you can cope with dramatic change, you are ready
for the first of Maryam's "signs."

A MARRIAGE AND MIRACULOUS WINE

We plunge straight into workshop mode with the story of a happening
at Kanah (Cana) as Sign One takes places at a wedding celebration.

(John 2:1–11) On the third day there was a wedding in Cana of
Galilee, and the mother of Jesus was there. Jesus and his disciples
had also been invited to the wedding. When the wine gave out, the
mother of Jesus said to him, "They have no wine." And Jesus said
to her, "Woman, what concern is that to you and to me? My hour
has not yet come." His mother said to the servants, "Do whatever
he tells you." Now standing there were six stone water jars for the
Jewish rites of purification, each holding twenty or thirty gallons.
Jesus said to them, "Fill the jars with water." And they filled them
up to the brim. He said to them, "Now draw some out, and take it
to the chief steward." So they took it. When the steward tasted the
water that had become wine, and did not know where it came from
(though the servants who had drawn the water knew), the steward
called the bridegroom and said to him, "Everyone serves the good
wine first, and then the inferior wine after the guests have become
drunk. But you have kept the good wine until now." Jesus did this,
the first of his signs, in Cana of Galilee, and revealed his glory; and
his disciples believed in him.

After three periods of time ("days"), we travel to the village of Kanah,
a center of healing and shamanic ritual in northern Galilee. We are
invited to a wedding. There is quite a crowd. According to custom
people wash themselves in the usual way. In the dreamlike atmosphere, we are told nothing about the couple or their family. We may
wonder if this is not a wedding in the usual sense, even though there
is no feeling of strangeness. Then, as we see Yeshua sitting away from
the wedding canopy, his mother appears and whispers in his ear. The
master of ceremonies has told her that the wine is running out. She
turns to Yeshua as if it were his responsibility. This is peculiar because
the fact that Yeshua is the groom has been omitted from the text.
Yet, if he is not the groom, why has the master of ceremonies turned
up like this? The story does not tell us. Instead, Yeshua laughs and

says: "That's not my concern, mother, and nothing for you to worry about either. Tell him we can drink fresh water." In a bizarre gesture for a Jewish person, he points toward the water jars, which were used for washing. Normally, people would not drink from those jars, but the master of ceremonies, without batting an eyelid, nods and directs the servants to decant water from the jars into pitchers. More dream scenario, but again, there is no feeling of strangeness as they begin to serve the guests and they drink, even though a Jew would never drink water that had been used for washing. People get up to dance. A man turns to his neighbor and shouts to the gathering that the best wine has been saved until now. The ablutions water has become the best wine. We assume that Yeshua has made this happen. He says nothing. He looks at us, smiles, and holds up one finger. We are told that this is a sign.

The image of the *sign* would take the listener/reader back to the first book of the Torah where God designates the rainbow as a sign of the divine covenant with the Creation (Genesis 9:8–17). God *is* the Creation. God *is* life. This first sign is about creation and life, the profound themes behind the ceremony and celebration of marriage. But is there further meaning in this first Sign?

WHAT DOES SIGN ONE MEAN TO YOU?

The wedding that we show to others, whether through ceremony or tacit agreement, is the outward sign of an inner reality—two become one in a sacred union. The invited guests have been chosen to witness that sign and to honor that inner reality. But, just as in a dream, the story says nothing about the marriage itself—who was getting married, for example—and instead describes a particular incident during the following celebrations. Just when everyone is enjoying themselves, the mother of Yeshua is told that the wine is running out. Why she was so anxious about this we do not know. She turns to her son to tell him, though it is not his responsibility. He is not concerned and suggests that everyone can drink water. But somehow the water has turned into wine. The structure of this bizarre chain of events tells us to pay attention and look for the hidden meaning. We realize that this lies in what has *not* been mentioned.

The ongoing speculation that the wedding was between Yeshua and Maryam leads us away from the point of Maryam's Story. In terms of the image of a wedding, they become one as far as the people are concerned. But they were already one. They came to the planet as twin souls with a joint mission. The followers would have already known that. Instead, Maryam is saying look behind the words, at the sign. This is the first sign on your pilgrimage. What does it say to you?

THE MEANING OF MARRIAGE

In the Semitic tradition, wedding is about holy balance, symbolized by the wedding canopy (*khupah* in Hebrew) under which the bride and groom enter into the covenant of marriage. The khupah also celebrates the inner marriage of each person with the Source. The symbol of the wedding celebration reminds us about the passage in the Gospel of Philip, which tells how Yeshua was always kissing Maryam. The mouth-to-mouth kiss between them, in the kiss of love, symbolizes the dynamic energy cycle in which there is an exchange of spirit as well as breath. As constant witness to their kissing, Yeshua's followers ask why he loves her more than them. Yeshua replies that when they can see with their inner eyes, they will have their answer, but until then they will be baffled (Gospel of Philip 66:55–56).

Records such as these are evidence that Yeshua did not come to planet Earth as a lone voice with a single message. The original message was delivered by Jesus and Mary Magdalene together. They were the embodiment of the two energy streams of Creation—the masculine and feminine—representing and living the sacred union of these energies. Their message was that we each have our own inner messiah—the presence of Oneness within, in the form of soul. We do not need an outer one. And Sign One tells us that the first step to revealing the inner messiah is to unite the two energy streams of the feminine and masculine within ourselves—whatever our gender—to realize that we are all One, and to let that realization help us deal with all the dualities outside us.

Both aspects of this twofold message have been rejected by Christianity so that we continue to depend on someone else, such as Jesus, for our "salvation," with the sole responsibility to live this dependency. The concept of sacred union and the sacred feminine was abandoned, plunging sex, sexuality, female blood, sensuality, the body, and everything to do with the natural world, into the dark realms of sinful necessity. The disastrous consequences for the individual and collective psyche of millions around the world, throughout nearly 2,000 years, are still with us. The twofold message was radical and revolutionary. At the dawn of the second millennium of the Common Era, it still falls on deaf ears as human beings cry out for inner liberation and nourishment for the soul.

START WITH ONENESS

Make the two one, Yeshua advises in the Gospel of Thomas (Log. 22). This is the basis of transformation, for there is only one reality and that is the spiritual reality of the sacred. When we realize and practice this, something changes within us as the reality of the soul emerges. Yeshua is laughing because he wonders whether we have really got the message, so he holds up a finger . . . all the seeming opposites in life are in fact one, for they all come from the Oneness. All the apparent opposites are seen and experienced by the personality as the oneness of life when perceived by the eye of the heart as a continuum. It is as if the red "water" that carries life itself, the blood, becomes ennobled. Maryam signals to us: from the beginning start with Oneness—with the fact that we are all one, that everything is one.

The sacred reality that we are all one has to be demonstrated in life. The theme of the wedding is where we have been taken. Here, all the opposites must be realized as one—the "two" become "one." In our own heart—referred to in the Gospel of Philip as the Bridal Chamber, the holy of holies—we must begin to realize that the world as we perceive it is a sacred unity. Maryam is saying that this is the first giant step that has to be made before we can go any further into her teachings. Now the words of Yeshua: "I and the Father (the Source) are one" have to be put into practice. Theoretically, you can love your neighbor as yourself because you are one. You can try. Questions are immediately brought up by your heart: But do I even like my neighbor, and do I really love myself? You may feel that the reply should be: Of course I do, that's why I'm on this journey. Then your heart reminds you that you do not yet *know* who you really are. In which case, who is it that is being loved? While we are pondering that one, we can look further into the wisdom of Sign One.

The celebrated Jewish philosopher, Martin Buber, considered that a relationship between two becomes holy when we see the divine in one another. When we see each other as objects that either help or harm us, we are not only blind to the holiness within everyone, we miss experiencing the Divine. Sacred marriage is about the duality of male and female being one. This is the mystery of the Bridal Chamber mentioned as a sacrament in the Gospel of Philip. The in-breath and out-breath are also symbolized in Jacob's vision of the ascending and descending "angels"—the energy of spirit being received and the energy of spirit being given back to the Source—the twofold flow of the one energy, the breath from heaven and the breath from Earth.

BALANCE BEGINS WITH WATER

Healing ecology concerns balance—the balance of our body, the balance of the communal body, the balance of the global body, and how these three are in balance with Nature. With Sign One we begin the process of balance. When Nature is out of balance, many of the problems that occur can be traced to water. Water is the elemental force that unlocks what lies dormant. Traditionally, she is one of the three Mothers of Creation and holds the balance between Air and Fire. She is the force that unlocks the hidden possibilities of seed, and on a spiritual level represents the force that unlocks our own personal potentials during our life journey. When water unlocks our deepest potentials, we can free ourselves from the bondage of our mindsets, conditioning, and other obstacles. But water alone cannot do this. Water must have the vital ingredient of life—hence the immersion in "living" waters. This is life as it is, without definitions and conditions. Recognition of our spiritual reality releases a universal life force into our lives, symbolized by the image of water turning to wine—the "waters" of our body and personality become ennobled.

When the Pharaoh of Egypt refused to let the Hebrews go, the life force left the various places of water and they became places of death (Exodus 7). In our own time, the life force is being driven out of the various places of water, including the oceans. We have to take action to bring back the life force before the waters become so unhealthy that they become places of death. It is important for us to realize what is happening and do our best to live in balance. Each of us can create rippling effects to help sweeten the lives of others and the life of our planet.

We pause now to recall that Maryam, as feminine archetype, embodies all the forces of water. Hence water, and what it represents, is a recurring theme of the transformational Story. But have we simply focused on the apparent miracle? The followers would have known that throughout first-century Palestine, there were magicians who could turn water into a range of things, including wine. The Rabbi is no magician. When he changes the nature of something, he is giving a teaching. He is not trying to impress. But that's what impressed the people. Some of them followed him because he could do things like that, outside of the dream story. It is we who have to change our conditioned nature, not someone else. We take up the role of magician: we do not leave it to someone else, nor do we expect it to be someone else. It is we who will change our nature.

THE ENNOBLING OF WATER

The transformation Story began with water. First, we were reminded of the creative Beginning where Light and the Holy Breath moved across the Waters. Living beings were created in this way, each being filled with the divine energy of the Source. Then history is convoluted, eons of earthly experience have gone by, and we are shown certain human creatures being immersed in water to wash away the "darkness"— negative energies—that they have accumulated during their lives. People also cleanse themselves with water before taking part in any sacred ceremony, such as a wedding. Later, after the revelation that two become one, that two always were one, water features again. But now it has been turned into the fermented juice of the grape, where light, heat, the soil, and its organisms have all played a part in creating wine. Energetic patterns have been transformed.

All energy is conscious since it originates from the one source of consciousness. Every being and every thing is made of the energy of the Source, creating a network of consciousness in which all beings and things are interconnected. Further, all things are actually in communion with all other things so that all changes are registered within the network of consciousness. These aspects of subtle energy physics are what enable the shaman-prophet—who is aligned with them—to bring about changes within physicality.

In Nature the elements of water, earth, air, and sunlight are united by the hidden activities of the vine, where the atomic components of water have not been simply rearranged, they have been transformed. Our inner understanding that all dualities are aspects of unity ennobles all forms of water in us so that they resemble wine. In energetic terms the blood has an increased capacity for carrying the subtle energy of the life force.

In the Bridal Chamber, in the exchange of bodily fluids, the "waters" of the two people merge. In sacred union, the marriage within, this happens on all levels. When a marriage is about this, then water truly becomes wine. In such a relationship two people can discover the meaning of the Bridal Chamber—how two do not simply reveal themselves as one, but the two can be a single, unique reality as the embodiment of unconditional love. Love, they discover, is the means by which people can let go of their conditioning and associated attachments to make space for the energy of spirit.

Yeshua and Maryam spoke Aramaic. The Aramaic word *damah*, "wine," also means "blood." Damah contains the root of the name given to the primordial human being, Adam. The creative, sexual, and erotic overtones of damah, in the context of a wedding, would not have been lost on Maryam's followers. The creative, the sexual, and the erotic in life all have the power to lead us to the meditative state and the blissful experience of oneness—they have within them the meaning of wedding. Perhaps an important transformational question to carry with us might be: How does the water of erotic love (Greek: *eros*) become the wine of unconditional love (*agapi*), and can the desire for another become the love for another? Perhaps they could be the same and is there any need to separate them?

WHO DOES THE ENNOBLING?

Looking behind Maryam's words, we also discover that as we encourage the flow of unconditional love, our emotional life (symbolized by water) is ennobled, and our body consciousness is ennobled through the conscious joining of our two energy streams. Maryam points to this in the curious exchange between Yeshua and his mother: "When the wine gave out, the mother of Jesus said to him, 'They have no wine.' And Jesus said to her, 'Woman, what concern is that to you and to me?'" Each of us has to do our own ennobling. It is no concern of either Yeshua or his mother.

But it seems that in the next moment he does interfere and creates the "miracle" that is "the first of his signs." In the Teaching Story such juxtapositions are deliberate. They are very much like the Zen koan that is designed to move the student out of the mind and into the heart. Maryam is prompting us to discover the fourth level of this mysterious and contradictory account. When we recall that in Maryam's Teaching Story, Yeshua is a symbol of the soul, the mist clears. It is the soul that does the ennobling. Your task, then, is to align yourself with your soul. And while we are on the subject, this is the alignment you will need to uncover the deep, fourth level wisdom of Maryam's Teaching Story.

ENTERING THE BRIDAL CHAMBER

Earlier in chapter 3, we saw how the Dialogue of the Savior was a text capable of plunging the listener/reader straight into fourth-level understanding. Like the Gospel of Philip, the Dialogue also talks of the Bridal Chamber, but we are into cosmic dimensions here. The text cautions that a person should enter it "clothed in light"—stripped of the ego-construct we think of as our reality. The Bridal Chamber is a metaphor for reconnection with the sacred by making the two energy streams one. Thus, the Bridal Chamber (the heart center) is the divine womb in which a new being is conceived.

TO SUM UP

UNITE ALL DUALITIES AND
PREPARE FOR "REBIRTH"

When the first Sign points to the concept of the wedding, the teaching is that the energy of the Source enters the physical realm as two streams, traditionally applied to the masculine and feminine genders. The masculine energy stream is, more accurately, the emissive stream—it moves outward. The feminine stream is receptive. Each of us, regardless of gender, embodies both energy streams, or we would not be human. The deeper meaning of the wedding, therefore, is the unity of the two energy streams within each human being. Here, marriage is about unity rather than any permutations of gender.

Through the experience of oneness, there is a spiritual birth whereby the person emerges reborn. In the teachings of Sign One, the hints and allusions about Maryam in the New Testament come together—she is concerned with coronation and death, but, more importantly, she is concerned with rebirth. Maryam's Sign One message is not heavy. Rebirth is always a cause for celebration.

Traditionally, wine is a symbol of wisdom. In Sign One we encounter the beginnings of wisdom, as well as the poet Blake's "wine of delight." The reference to the guests becoming "drunk" is saying that you should celebrate the ennobling of your "waters" as a joyous thing. And from now on, when the recurring subject of water comes up, listen out for the splash of people having fun.

How Is Your Body?

It is time to listen to the wisdom of the body. Maryam's references and allusions to the primordial human being, Adam, and to the blood and the waters of the body, bring us to a memorable story where our vision of our body as something to house the "us" is revised. During its sojourn on Earth, the soul seeks to express its divine origin through the vehicle of our physical body and our personality. Our souls come to take part in creating a heaven on Earth. This is what my beach vision showed me. Life does not have to be created solely via the reactions of our conditioned minds, as it has been for millennia. If we did not pick it up at the opening of Maryam's Teaching Story, in the following episode she is saying that we can begin the process of change by realizing that our body, this "house," is actually a sacred place, a temple, and that we need to treat it, and all the other "temples," as such.

♦ ───

(John 2:12–22) After this he went down to Capernaum with his mother, his brothers, and his disciples; and they remained there a few days. The Passover of the Jews was near, and Jesus went up to Jerusalem. In the temple he found people selling cattle, sheep, and doves, and the money changers seated at their tables. Making a whip of cords, he drove all of them out of the temple, both the sheep and the cattle. He also poured out the coins of the money changers and overturned their tables. He told those who were selling the doves, "Take these things out of here! Stop making my Father's house a marketplace!" His disciples remembered that it was written, "Zeal for your house will consume me." The Jews then said to him, "What sign can you show us for doing this?" Jesus answered them, "Destroy this temple, and in three days I will raise it up." The Jews then said, "This temple has been under construction for forty-six years, and will you raise it up in three days?" But he was speaking of the temple of his body. After he was raised from the dead, his disciples remembered that he had said this; and they believed the scripture and the word that Jesus had spoken.

No one seems to notice when Yeshua and Maryam and a few close friends leave the wedding. Camels are waiting and they travel to K'far Nakhum (Capernaum), by the water. They stay there a few days until the pilgrimage festival of Pesakh (Passover), commemorating the escape of the Hebrews from Egyptian bondage. In common with Jews of the time, Yeshua decides to make pilgrimage back south to Judea, to the Jerusalem Temple. Maryam's account of the so-called cleansing of the temple does not tally with the chronology of the other three canonical gospels (Matthew 21:12–17; Mark 11:15–19; Luke 19:45–48) where the incident is preceded by Yeshua riding into Jerusalem on a donkey. In the accounts by the other three gospel writers, the whole affair was the last straw for the Temple officials, especially Kayafah (Caiaphas) the high priest, and undoubtedly led to Yeshua's later arrest. Apart from some probable later inserts, the other three canonical gospels choose to link the Temple incident with the Crucifixion and Resurrection so that the new Christian event of Easter neatly takes the place of the Jewish Passover.

But Maryam recounts the rumble in the Temple at this point in her transformation story for a special reason: as a sequel to Sign One and a preliminary to our engagement with Sign Two. Her followers would have noted that she does not link the Passover with the torture and death of her soul mate, Yeshua; rather, she preserves the meaning of Pesakh and the meaning of the Temple and temple cleansing.

This is the first of three times that Yeshua goes to Jerusalem for the Passover celebrations. Maryam's listeners would immediately recall that she is talking about a release from bondage. Of course they know that her transformation story is designed to help release them from the bondage of not experiencing their divine reality, but she will shortly go further to look at what actually is a state of bondage.

We leave a beautiful place of water and trek south to Jerusalem, only to find when we get to the Temple that the courtyard resembles a marketplace, teeming with people buying and selling. The sight of this sacred building being used for trade enrages Yeshua. As he sets about clearing the site, the gospels of Mark, Matthew, and Luke have him quoting the words of the shaman-prophet Isaiah. But Maryam's account is far more relevant and moving, for, in the minds of his followers, it is as if Yeshua shouts: "Zeal for your house will consume me!" These are words from Psalm 69, a petition from an individual lamenting the destruction of the Temple and describing how he is drowning in the hatred of those within his own society. As we have seen, Maryam's transformation story is interwoven with regular references to the Jewish scriptures, suggesting that her followers at the time were mainly Jews. She is reminding them about who they are and the great ancestral tradition that goes ahead of them like a richly laden caravan. The Semitic concept of history means that at any time in the present, we may join the "caravan" of our ancestors, travel to any part of it, and benefit from the wisdom of previous travelers. The past becomes now.

Straight after the Temple drama, Maryam subtly alerts us to the crux of her account with the word *sign*. Yeshua is surrounded by a crowd of Judeans (Jews) and someone angrily demands: "What sign can you show us for doing this?" If he is not one of the Temple officials, what right has he got for creating such a rumpus; what are his credentials? Yeshua's baffling response is to compare the fabric of the sacred space with his own body. Maryam's sign is pointing to *physical bodies!*

With the word house (*bet*), Maryam directs our attention back to "in the beginning" (b'reshit). At this point in our journey, it is time to look carefully at our body. As the sacred vehicle for the soul's expression, it is a temple indeed. But do we see it like that, do we treat it like that, do we look after it like that, and, furthermore, how do we look upon the bodies of others? Is a body just another object to be exploited? A little earlier in this story, we left a beautiful place of water to get to this awakening about the body. Water, symbolizing the emotions, takes us to the heart where a message awaits us.

TO SUM UP
WHAT ARE BODIES?

At this early stage on the journey, we are cautioned to carefully consider how we are using the sacred vehicle of our body and if we are in a state of bondage of any kind with regard to our body and the way we think and act. Our lifestyle may already be telling us about this. And if our motive for pilgrimage is about some kind of gain or exploitation, we have missed the point and forgotten what the "temple" is for. We may never have realized that our body has its own wisdom, or we may have lost touch with the wisdom of the body.

In Aramaic, Hebrew, and Greek, wisdom is a feminine force. Both Hebrew scripture and Maryam's story say that it is this feminine force that creates every soul, every being. We may recall that Maryam embodies this force within herself. But she would go further to ask us to realize that the feminine energy stream within each of us is an embodiment of Sophia, the wisdom who brings about the creation of the new. This should cause us to look at ourselves with new eyes. Our readiness to engage with Sign Two is being tested as Maryam gives us this opportunity to regroup.

Our attitude to our physical body and the bodies of others is one of the necessary preliminaries of regrouping. A second concern is our physical body and the emotional, mental, and spiritual levels of our selves as they feature in Yeshua's enigmatic concept of being born again.

BEING BORN AGAIN

(John 3:1–13) Now there was a Pharisee named Nicodemus, a leader of the Jews. He came to Jesus by night and said to him, "Rabbi, we know that you are a teacher who has come from God; for no one can do these signs that you do apart from the presence of God." Jesus answered him, "Very truly, I tell you, no one can see the kingdom of God without being born from above." Nicodemus said to him, "How can anyone be born after having grown old? Can one enter a second time into the mother's womb and be born?" Jesus answered, "Very truly, I tell you, no one can enter the kingdom of God without being born of water and Spirit. What is born of the flesh is flesh, and what is born of the Spirit is spirit. Do not be astonished that I said to you, 'You must be born from above.' The wind blows where it chooses, and you hear the sound of it, but you do not know where it comes from or where it goes. So it is with everyone who is born of the Spirit." Nicodemus said to him, "How can these things be?" Jesus answered him, "Are you a teacher of Israel, and yet you do not understand these things? Very truly, I tell you, we speak of what we know and testify to what we have seen; yet you do not receive our testimony. If I have told you about earthly things and you do not believe, how can you believe if I tell you about heavenly things? No one has ascended into heaven except the one who descended from heaven, the Son of Man."

In the next scene we camp outside the city for the night. After sunset someone enters the camp looking for Yeshua. Perhaps the approaching person does not want others to know what he is doing and decides to seek out Yeshua under cover of darkness. We can be sure that the time of day has been carefully chosen by Maryam. This is when campfires would be lit, songs sung, dances danced, stories told, and culture passed on. Reference to nighttime, with its changes of light and changes of atmosphere, is often used in storytelling to signal something special or secret, a change from the everyday to the magical.

THE PROBLEM FOR NICODEMUS

His name is Nakdimon (Latin: Nicodemus), a well-known teacher of the Parushim (Pharisees). Like all Pharisees, Nicodemus enjoys debating points of law and religion. Like Levi, the tax collector, he is rich and gives large amounts of money to the Temple. Tonight he has something on his mind. Nicodemus says he knows Yeshua is a holy person because of his reputation as a healer. He has also heard how Yeshua insists that everyone is capable of healing others. He is intrigued. "How can I be like you?" he asks. Yeshua looks at him carefully. Nicodemus is unnerved by this. "First, you will need to be born again," says Yeshua. Nicodemus wonders if he is a fake. "Is that all you have to say? How can a person be born twice? You can't get back into your mother's womb." Yeshua laughs at the idea. "No, of course you can't. First you were born of water. Now you must be born of the spirit of life. I'm talking about a different kind of birth." Here is an echo of the earlier mention about immersion. First we need to be immersed in the waters of life, then, having let go of the negative energies associated with our past, we need to be immersed in the *spirit* of life, to make contact with the source of life itself.

A MAN OF GOD

"You are a teacher who has come from God. No one can do these signs that you do apart from the presence of God."

Nicodemus's choice of words would have evoked in Maryam's listeners the stories of their ancestral wonder-working teachers, like Elijah who was known as a "man of God" (1 Kings 17). This is someone who can intercede with God (or the spirit world) on behalf of those who need healing help. The signs mentioned by Nicodemus point to divine presence, and this is what has got him wondering about Yeshua.

BORN FROM THE BEGINNING

The confusion in the mind of the Pharisee is more easily understood in Maryam's language of Aramaic where she has Yeshua using the phrase *min d'rish,* "born from the beginning." Nicodemus misunderstands this to mean to be born again from his mother's womb. But this is an echo that presents Maryam's listeners once again with the Creation story.

She is emphasizing that we are always creating who we are, but the trick is to be conscious of this. Nicodemus represents those of us who do not realize that we are co-creators of life, with the source of life. He knows that a Jew acknowledges the One who gives life, but he is baffled by the idea of being born twice in the same lifetime. Yeshua repeats the teaching that you have to go back to your own Beginning, to create yourself anew. This is a spiritual rebirth where you experience the presence of Oneness as yourself. But, Yeshua asks, if he has a problem with these facts of earthly life, how would he be able to grasp what Yeshua could tell him about the life of the spirit?

The Pharisee, representing the letter of the Law and scriptural authority, is challenged. He has come this far and he has done well. Yet, to be a healer like Yeshua, it seems he must go back to the beginning. The trappings of his religion that he holds dear are of no use if they do not lead a person to experience the Oneness. Will he dare to follow this truth? What is at stake here? Nicodemus is amazed and compares Yeshua's teaching with what he has been brought up to believe. Is this what others have been teaching outside Jerusalem—that people experience the presence of Oneness as themselves? He feels fear in his stomach. How can this be? He wonders whether to tell other Pharisees or keep the conversation to himself, for his dilemma is further exacerbated by Yeshua's final words about the "son of man."

WHAT IS A "SON OF MAN"?

This phrase has been interpreted for centuries to align with the Christian dogma that Yeshua is talking about himself as the savior Godman. In Aramaic, however, the common term for human being was "son of man," or even "son of God"; after all this is merely a description of what human beings actually are. Yeshua is making a very important point here—we are *all* spiritual beings. Yeshua, Maryam, and the rest of us have all come into incarnation from the realm of spirit and, as souls, this is to where we return. We come here to express the sacred through the vehicle of the physical body and our personality. Part of being born again is grasping this reality. Since people tend to forget this, advanced human beings, such as Yeshua and Maryam, have been incarnating on this planet on a regular basis to remind us.

BORN OF WATER

At the beginning we found ourselves watching John the Baptizer immersing people in the living waters of the river in a ritual of cleansing. The conversation between Yeshua and Nicodemus confirms the importance for us of this person John and what he represents. "Born of water" takes us back to the maternal womb where the incarnating soul was first immersed in a liquid. In order to become a living individual, the life force, the spirit, enters the new being. Thus the new being is born of water and the spirit. It is alive. We are alive, but we may not be aware of how that is.

The new research about Mary Magdalene, initiated by the discovery of the Nag Hammadi texts, reveals that she was the carrier of a shamanic tradition that can be traced back through the teachings of Yeshua and John to the esoteric teachings of Judaism, to the Egyptian and Sumerian mysteries of Isis, Inanna, and the dream goddess Nanshe, and to the Earth-based source of all religions. Maryam knows about the journey of the soul. This is made clear in the Pistis Sophia, the Dialogue of the Savior, and the Gospel of Mary (Magdalene). She knows what being born again is all about.

Immersion is still a tradition for Jews undergoing life changes. Energetically, ceremonial immersion in "living waters"—usually those of a river or lake—washes away and cleanses the past or the accumulation of negative energies. What you think of as your past is your own construct from your reactions to the way you have been nurtured and influenced by your life so far. You wish to start with a new vision of reality, untainted by the mindsets, conditioning, and prejudices that you have accumulated so far, in order to experience your reality and the reality of being. Maryam has given us a clue to another layer of understanding about immersion in living waters. By "washing away" previous conditioning and notions about the purpose of Earth life, we can be creative and make a fresh start.

Next, you are asked to realize your connection to the Earth and Nature, as the unveiled face of God—how they are sacred—and to become aware of the cycle of energy from Spirit to the physical and back to Spirit. There is no place in this cycle that is not sacred since all is Spirit in some form. Each one of us is on a journey and we can all learn from each other. Every time we let go of old conditioning, we acquire a little more freedom to express the soul.

WE ARE PEOPLE OF LIGHT

In Italian, to give birth is *dare alla luce,* "to give to the light"—a beautiful reminder that the incarnating soul comes into the light of Earth life from the darkness of the womb cave. Further, the light of spirit is not just in some realm other than Earth. Every incarnating soul brings the light of spirit with it as a gift to the universe and life on planet Earth. As the Polish eco-philosopher Henryk Skolimowski, puts it: "We are all truly one because we are all made of Light." Maryam reminds us that it is only our clouded vision that prevents us from realizing this. And with this realization, nothing will be the same again. But this experience cannot be bought. Each of us has to make the effort to raise our consciousness to that level of understanding.

TO SUM UP

NEW RELATIONSHIPS ARE CALLED FOR

There are other ways in which we need to be born again. We are not yet healed. To be healed we must be reborn out of the pain of our past and accept the new life that begins now. This new life depends on our entering into new relationships.

Maryam had to move on from the grief of Yeshua's death to a new life without his *physical* presence. She was able to do this because she was given proof that love is a spiritual energy that does not die when a person gives up his physical body. The true love bond is never broken. As many of the Gnostic scriptures show, this meant a new relationship with Yeshua, which still allowed her to carry on the teachings of the movement. We are offered a similar challenge—to begin a new relationship with Maryam in her spiritual form and us in our physical form—so that we can go on to live her teachings.

We can guess that at this point in Maryam's story, Yeshua is smiling. He looks at us and nods.

THE WOMAN AT THE WELL

(John 3:22; 4:1–42) After this Jesus and his disciples went into
the Judean countryside, and he spent some time there with them
and baptized. Now when Jesus learned that the Pharisees had
heard, "Jesus is making and baptizing more disciples than John"—
although it was not Jesus himself but his disciples who baptized—
he left Judea and started back to Galilee. But he had to go through
Samaria. So he came to a Samaritan city called Sychar, near the
plot of ground that Jacob had given to his son Joseph. Jacob's well
was there, and Jesus, tired out by his journey, was sitting by the
well. It was about noon. A Samaritan woman came to draw water,
and Jesus said to her, "Give me a drink." (His disciples had gone to
the city to buy food.) The Samaritan woman said to him, "How is
it that you, a Jew, ask a drink of me, a woman of Samaria?" (Jews
do not share things in common with Samaritans.) Jesus answered
her, "If you knew the gift of God, and who it is that is saying to
you, 'Give me a drink,' you would have asked him, and he would
have given you living water." The woman said to him, "Sir, you
have no bucket, and the well is deep. Where do you get that living
water? Are you greater than our ancestor Jacob, who gave us the
well, and with his sons and his flocks drank from it?" Jesus said to
her, "Everyone who drinks of this water will be thirsty again, but
those who drink of the water that I will give them will never be
thirsty. The water that I will give will become in them a spring of
water gushing up to eternal life." The woman said to him, "Sir, give
me this water, so that I may never be thirsty or have to keep coming here to draw water." Jesus said to her, "Go, call your husband,
and come back." The woman answered him, "I have no husband."
Jesus said to her, "You are right in saying, 'I have no husband';
for you have had five husbands, and the one you have now is not
your husband. What you have said is true!" The woman said to

him, "Sir, I see that you are a prophet. Our ancestors worshiped on this mountain, but you say that the place where people must worship is in Jerusalem." Jesus said to her, "Woman, believe me, the hour is coming when you will worship the Father neither on this mountain nor in Jerusalem. You worship what you do not know; we worship what we know, for salvation is from the Jews. But the hour is coming, and is now here, when the true worshipers will worship the Father in spirit and truth, for the Father seeks such as these to worship him. God is spirit, and those who worship him must worship in spirit and truth." The woman said to him, "I know that Messiah is coming (who is called Christ). When he comes, he will proclaim all things to us." Jesus said to her, "I am he, the one who is speaking to you." Just then his disciples came. They were astonished that he was speaking with a woman, but no one said, "What do you want?" or, "Why are you speaking with her?" Then the woman left her water jar and went back to the city. She said to the people, "Come and see a man who told me everything I have ever done! He cannot be the Messiah, can he?" They left the city and were on their way to him. Meanwhile the disciples were urging him, "Rabbi, eat something." But he said to them, "I have food to eat that you do not know about." So the disciples said to one another, "Surely no one has brought him something to eat?" Jesus said to them, "My food is to do the will of him who sent me and to complete his work. Do you not say, 'Four months more, then comes the harvest?' But I tell you, look around you, and see how the fields are ripe for harvesting. The reaper is already receiving wages and is gathering fruit for eternal life, so that sower and reaper may rejoice together. For here the saying holds true, 'One sows and another reaps.' I sent you to reap that for which you did not labor. Others have labored, and you have entered into their labor." Many Samaritans from that city believed in him because of the woman's testimony, "He told me everything I have ever done." So when the Samaritans came to him, they asked him to stay with them; and he stayed there two days. And many more believed because of his word. They said to the woman, "It is no longer because of what you said that we believe, for we have heard for ourselves, and we know that this is truly the Savior of the world."

After striking camp the Yeshua party moves out into the Judean countryside near the River Jordan. We have already understood that John has been cleansing people through ritual immersion and that some of them would have been prepared in this way to meet with the new Rabbi, Yeshua. In other words their consciousness has been raised or awakened to what Yeshua has to offer in terms of a fresh vision of life for them. Some of Yeshua's followers may have been involved in these rituals, but Yeshua also brings a revolutionary form of baptism—baptism by the spirit or holy breath.

This is a dream story, but the length of the episode tells us that it is no mere interlude. Maryam stops us here to underline some important teachings before we arrive in the Galilee. You may wonder, as I have done, that since the disciples had gone into the town to buy food, who was there by the well to record Yeshua's strangely cryptic conversation with the Samaritan woman? The answer is almost certainly Maryam, for Jewish listeners would have found it strange for a lone Samaritan woman, or even a Jewish woman, to approach a strange man on his own.

HANGING OUT IN SAMARIA

Yeshua did not have to go through Samaria, despite what was written in John 4:4. The normal route north from Jerusalem would not take Jews through Samaria because the Samaritans, though ethnically and religiously related, were regarded by the Judeans as pariahs. The phrase "Jews do not share things in common with Samaritans" is a polite way of stating the situation. This was true for Judeans but many Galileans found no problem in mixing with Samaritans, and traveling north through Samaria would have made the journey shorter. Even so, it was highly unusual for the group to rest up for two days in a Samaritan mountain village instead of somewhere nearer the normal camel road.

Why do they choose this particular route? Who is this Samaritan woman, and what is the purpose of the story? From the point of view of later Christian redactors, the story is used to further emphasize the message that Jesus is the Messiah/Christ, but as it stands the story does not support this message. There are many obvious anomalies, such as the contradictory statement that Jesus either was or was not baptizing people (see John 3:22 and 4:2). When he tells the Samaritan woman about her previous partners, Yeshua is simply demonstrating the psychic ability, common to many wandering healers and teachers at the time, to read a person's energy field. It would not have caused people to leave the town and come out to meet the alleged messiah. We will need to look behind the words of the conversation.

JACOB'S WELL

The party had stopped outside the mountain town of Shekhem (Sychar), near the piece of land that the ancestral patriarch Jacob gave to his son Yosef. The well in the Story was known as Jacob's Well. Again, we are with the theme of water, and the Jewish patriarch who dreamed about the cyclic movement of divine energies. This well is a good place for "God-wrestlers" to stop and take a breather. Public wells were virtually exclusive to women, who went there to draw water and to socialize with other females. Listeners of the time would have also picked up on the theme of the well, recalling that Maryam's ancient namesake, Miriam, also had a well named after her. Maryam is indeed the well from which her followers, thirsting for spiritual wisdom, may drink. Maryam's Teaching Story is the well that she still offers us, as pilgrim travelers.

We would have been well fed and watered at the wedding ceremony in Sign One. Here in the safe haven of a mountain village house, we can take stock of what we have learned about food as well as drink. Having jogged our memories about wells and all that they mean to a desert wanderer, Maryam carefully builds the Samaritan episode to its surprising climax.

SPIRITUAL DRINK AND
SPIRITUAL NOURISHMENT

A woman has appeared. Perhaps she has something to tell us about the feminine. Maryam alerts us to this possibility when she has Yeshua opening a conversation with the Samaritan woman, beginning with some seemingly innocent phrases about water before suddenly assuring the woman that he has a special kind of water to offer. While we are pondering on the significance of this, Yeshua appears to change the subject when he asks her to call her husband. But this request sets in motion a train of understanding that will take us to the wisdom embedded in this episode.

The Samaritan woman realizes that Yeshua can see into her heart. In effect he says: "If you've already had five husbands, what have you been looking for? You are looking for what I can give you—'water' to quench your thirst for love and a spiritual answer." Yeshua's declaration addresses the fact that people search outside themselves because they feel incomplete. They think that if they can only find the right "other," they will be complete, instead of first uniting the two energy streams within themselves and only then joining with a partner. Yeshua is saying that the water of spiritual nourishment does not have to be drawn from a well and hauled back to your house. It is available all the time.

This theme is further developed when the disciples ask Yeshua to eat. "I already have food that you don't know about: spiritual food. Like spiritual water, you can have spiritual food all the time. But you have to wait for physical food. You can't have it until you've tilled the ground, sown the seed, and reaped the harvest. You cannot even get a loaf without thinking about this process."

Yeshua, as the soul in Maryam's dream Story, is saying that spiritual nourishment is as vital as physical food and drink. Phrases like "a thirst for knowledge," and "a hunger for truth," remind us that the quest for our spirituality is a natural need because we are sacred beings. It is as natural as the search for food and drink because it is part of our human makeup. We don't have to wait for the time when the Messiah makes an appearance because the time is here. We each have an inner messiah: the I AM as soul, right now.

HOLY PLACES

As a new understanding begins to dawn in the Samaritan woman, she wonders where the proper place to worship God might be.

(John 4:19–24) The woman said to him, "Sir, I see that you are a prophet. Our ancestors worshiped on this mountain, but you say that the place where people must worship is in Jerusalem." Jesus said to her, "Woman, believe me, the hour is coming when you will worship the Father neither on this mountain nor in Jerusalem. You worship what you do not know; we worship what we know, for salvation is from the Jews. But the hour is coming, and is now here, when the true worshipers will worship the Father in spirit and truth, for the Father seeks such as these to worship him. God is spirit, and those who worship him must worship in spirit and truth."

Yeshua knows that one of the sacred Hebrew names of God is HaMakom, "The Place." Here they are at the well of Jacob, the scriptural figure who realized that everywhere on Earth was sacred. There is no place that is not the Godsource, so that one place cannot be more sacred than another, any more than one person can be more holy than another.

HOLDING UP A MIRROR

In John 4:25–26, "The woman said to him, 'I know that Messiah is coming (who is called Christ). When he comes, he will proclaim all things to us.' Jesus said to her, 'I am he, the one who is speaking to you.'"

As we now appreciate, the phrase "I AM" would alert Maryam's followers with its deep meaning. Yeshua is talking about the I AM Presence within himself. The Messiah is not somewhere else, or on his way, the Messiah is right here in front of you, in me and also in *you;* the same I AM that was revealed to Moses. The I AM is our true identity. Throughout his teaching life, Yeshua held up a mirror to the world. If you see the I AM in me, it is because you have the I AM within you.

WOMEN IN THE MOVEMENT AND THE PROBLEMS OF SEGREGATION

While you ponder that heartwarming fact, you need to decide if you are ready to accept some important and revolutionary points that Maryam is making about her followers and the Jesus movement. Women are not only welcomed but respected as equals and are able, as the story reveals, intuitively to recognize a great spiritual teacher.

To understand why Maryam tells this story as a follow-up to Sign One (making two into one), we have to remember that a Jewish man of the time would have avoided contact with both women and Samaritans. But Yeshua sees beyond gender, ethnicity, and social standing to a manifestation of I AM that is also himself. Through her narration of the long conversation between Yeshua and the Samaritan woman, Maryam assures her followers that she is not concerned about a person's gender, mode of life, or past life, since the reality is that we are all One.

This answers the Samaritan woman's question: "How is it that you, a Jew, ask a drink of me, a woman of Samaria?" But Maryam wants to address the problem of segregation that was current everywhere in the Middle East. And lo, two millennia later, segregation still occurs everywhere in the world. One group has its reasons for not sharing with another group. Worse, one group has its reasons for hating and even destroying another.

We are asked to take an honest look into our hearts to see whether our own mind-set is stuck in the past, with our prejudices and conditioning creating our present. Recalling the teachings of Sign One, have we realized that our own feminine energy stream is one half of our energetic makeup, no matter what our sexuality or gender may be? Or have we managed to separate ourselves from half our total being? The meeting of the feminine and masculine is a natural process. The two energy streams cannot be united, or restricted, according to the rules and regulations of others. There are no barriers to the meeting other than those imposed by religion, society, culture, and fear-based personal prejudice.

TO SUM UP

ARE YOU READY?

In her Teaching Story, when Maryam has Yeshua happy to be served by a Samaritan woman and happy to drink from a Samaritan well, she looks to her followers to follow this example. Her timeless message is that any form of segregation is missing the point. Any form of segregation, for whatever reason, cannot fit with the teaching that we are all One. It shows a failure to respect the divine nature of another soul and will inevitably lead to injustice and conflict. Back in her time and today in our time, we can see how certain individuals and groups use segregation for their own ends. They have missed the point of human existence. They do not know why they came to planet Earth, and they are terrified of where they might be going.

The Samaritan woman, symbolizing the feminine, gets the message: the I AM is within you and every person. Later, the townsfolk of Shekhem get it too because they are ready for it. Once Yeshua made the truth accessible, it made sense to them. This is why Maryam tells the story about a stopover in Samaria. When there is no separation between you and your heart, between you and I AM, you are ready to be nourished by the message of Holy Wisdom. The story of the Samaritan woman at the well of Jacob, like every aspect of Maryam's wisdom teachings, is about liberation and its healing power.

11

Sign Two

DISTANT HEALING, HUMILITY, AND THE LAST RESORT

Before we look at what the second dream is teaching, we need to address any night of mental confusion or emotional turmoil—the Nicodemus within—for such a night is fertile ground and so an important experience for us. The world that we perceive arises from the undifferentiated energy before the Creation. In any chaotic dream you might have had at this point in the journey, you are seeing the sacred energy before birth. It is unrecognizable to you and you find it disturbing. You have already presented yourself with the images of birth and rebirth as if your healing will be about such an event—the event that Yeshua considered essential. There is nothing to fear from such dreams. They simply show how you are prepared for the event from the very beginning. You begin with the chaos to be found within you as a result of emotions such as grief and anger. They can be harnessed as a creative force; the challenge is to reconcile yourself to the chaos within.

Our dreams are often like riddles, in the same way that illness and distress of the body, mind, or emotions can seem like riddles. The riddle cannot be solved by thinking alone. We need to somehow "think" with the heart and call upon the wisdom of the soul for a solution. Connection with the soul draws the core affliction into our consciousness, bringing both the affliction and the encounter with the sacred out of the darkness of the unconscious into the light of awareness. This is what is going to happen in the next episode of Maryam's Story.

◆──

(John 4:43–54) When the two days were over, he went from that place to Galilee (for Jesus himself had testified that a prophet has no honor in the prophet's own country). When he came to Galilee, the Galileans welcomed him, since they had seen all that he had done in Jerusalem at the festival; for they too had gone to the festival. Then he came again to Cana in Galilee where he had changed the water into wine. Now there was a royal official whose son lay ill in Capernaum. When he heard that Jesus had come from Judea to Galilee, he went and begged him to come down and heal his son, for he was at the point of death. Then Jesus said to him, "Unless you see signs and wonders you will not believe." The official said to him, "Sir, come down before my little boy dies." Jesus said to him, "Go; your son will live." The man believed the word that Jesus spoke to him and started on his way. As he was going down, his slaves met him and told him that his child was alive. So he asked them the hour when he began to recover, and they said to him, "Yesterday at one in the afternoon the fever left him." The father realized that this was the hour when Jesus had said to him, "Your son will live." So he himself believed, along with his whole household. Now this was the second sign that Jesus did after coming from Judea to Galilee.

Yeshua, the prophet, leaves Samaria where he had just been honored as "the Savior of the world," because a prophet has no honor in the prophet's own country! But, as we see in the very next verse, he is also honored in his own country of the Galilee. The two verses (also found in Matthew 13:57, Mark 6:4, and Luke 4:24) have obviously been doctored by later redactors so that they no longer make sense.

The day Yeshua and his party reach Kanah, an official of Herod's happens to be in the town. He lives in K'far Nakhum (Capernaum) where his son is very ill. Since Herod's spies are everywhere, this official knows that Yeshua is nearby. He sets off up the road with his bodyguards and meets the group of travelers. He hates to ask for help from the wandering rabbi but he is desperate. "You are the healer everyone's talking about. I beg you to come and help my little son. I don't want him to die." Yeshua knows the man would have him arrested if he could, but he needs a wonder-worker to save his son. The traveling group rests by the wayside. They have not seen this court official in such a state before.

Yeshua turns to the official and his bodyguards. "So you believe in miracles and wonders, but you do not believe in our teachings do you? You do not really believe in the love of the Holy One." The official is confused. He could lose his precious son and heir. "Please help me," he wails. Yeshua is thinking of the innocent child and wants to be rid of the hypocrite, but he also knows that he needs to be on good terms with the authorities in the Galilee. More than this, in spite of any front that they may be presenting or representing, he is able to see the divine reality of another person. He sits down quietly for a moment, ignoring the official's agitation. Then he looks at the official. "Go home," he says. "Your son is healed." The look on the official's face is enough to make the followers burst out laughing, but Yeshua simply smiles. The official does a bit more groveling and then he and his party rush off back down the road. He meets some of his house slaves coming toward him. "Master, it's all right. Your son has recovered. The fever left him a while ago."

The official does not send anyone back to thank Yeshua. Instead he makes a calculation in his mind. He realizes that his son must have come out of the fever about the time Yeshua said the boy was healed. His elation slowly turns to anxiety. Yeshua was right about him. In his heart he did not believe in healing. He is frightened by the fact of possibility. What else might this healer be able to do? Somehow, as often happens in a dreamlike story, everyone in the traveling group knows the boy has recovered. Yeshua holds up his hand as if to bless them, raising his first two fingers.

Like many traveling healers of the time, Yeshua can heal at a distance. But he is sorry that some people only turn to him for help when they are in trouble. They want the healing, but they do not want the spiritual message that healing conveys. Yeshua knows that healing is always possible because we are all One. He also shows the followers that their healing ministry can include working at a distance. The healer never discriminates, and in this healing modality, time and distance are no objects. The love of the Holy One falls, like rain, on everyone, no matter what their role in life might be. Maryam has alerted us with her signal, the word *sign*. It is time to ponder why this dream of distant healing occurs at this place on our journey.

YOU, THE DISTANT HEALER

Perhaps you may be asked to heal at a distance. You know that it is possible. Traditionally, the apprentice must learn about and practice distant healing before attempting "hands-on" work. Mastery of this form develops confidence as well as demonstrating profound truths about the nature of healing energies. The state of nonduality, as discovered in Sign One, means that you and the person needing your help are one. This is what makes the power of healing possible, and it is why distance, in either time or space, no longer affects the outcome. Have you got this?

You as healer are never alone. In the Semitic healing tradition, there are four angelic presences—four aspects of El. The angels are with you, the healer, whenever you request their presence. The angel Uriel shows both healer, and the person needing help, what is in front of them; Rafael presides over the act of healing; Mikhael embodies the wisdom, the energetic consciousness, of healing; and Gavriel offers post-healing support. Healing consciousness is consciousness of this reality.

Maryam had this consciousness. You may recall that knowledge of the All was one of the later Gnostic ways of describing such a consciousness. Maryam has this gnosis and she can initiate you into the power of distant healing.

HEALING OUR CHILDHOOD PAST

From early childhood most of us begin to lose spiritual consciousness as we become more and more immersed in physical life and conditioned by the words and behaviors of others as well as our own reactions to them. Healing is often needed from childhood onward, for this is when the illusion of separation from our spiritual origins—delivered to children by their parents, caregivers, and the world—begins to take hold and where the separation may already be manifesting as illness.

Healing childhood trauma involves returning to and healing the original wound. To reach this deep wound, we are dealing with the spiritual realities behind what has happened to us in our individual lives. Healing can take a person back to the time frame of the original trauma, to the time when disconnection from the sacred began to occur or was caused by some event.

Life does not have to be the way it appears to be. We can become individuals freed from the mind-sets thrust on us by religion, society, culture, political systems, or sets of beliefs, even though many may see this new person as a threat to the continuity of their power and control.

TRAUMA AS INITIATION

Sometimes a life-threatening condition suffered during our early years may in fact be a shamanic initiation that can stimulate the activity of the subtle energy centers (chakras) to enhance access to spiritual reality. The celebrated founder of anthroposophy, Rudolf Steiner, believed that most of the illnesses that Western children are now inoculated against were vital because they played a major role in helping to activate the subtle energy centers. He also believed that the soul played a part in initiating childhood illness or other trauma.

At any age illness or other trauma may be the catalyst for making life changes and to start really living. Illness gives us the opportunity to consider what is important in our lives, to follow our dreams, to heal old wounds, and perhaps to say goodbye. Illness or trauma empowers the soul to be heard and show us the way to a more fulfilling life. When we can see that everything is a form of love, we become happy with our life and everything in it. Then true healing has occurred, regardless of whether our physical bodies are ill or even dying.

HEALING SEPARATION

In terms of being, there is actually no past or future—only now—so we can make ancestral, as well as spirit, connections at any time. This is how memories connecting us to previous energetic patterns can exist in the now. We also carry within us patterns from our physical lineage, from the family, from our own spiritual lineage, and from our souls. Much healing involves changing the energies in some of these patterns. In spiritual healing patterns are first addressed at a soul level before the energies of healing can make the necessary changes in the mental, emotional, and physical levels. This means that healing is greatly enhanced when the person is willing and open to the sacred dimension of healing. Very often our ill health or distress can be traced to the struggle of the body and mind to be aligned with the soul. When this alignment is in place, we tend to be in good health.

LIVING AT ONE WITH THE WORLD

Healing our separation from the sacred presents us with a fundamental truth of being. We will have the opportunity to live this oneness, a demand far greater than a mere acknowledgment. Furthermore, because of our oneness with all beings, our good health is linked to the good health of the Earth and the Earth family. Thus, true healing cannot happen for human beings while the other beings of the Earth are being exploited, ravaged, desecrated, or made extinct by human behavior. Like us, all beings existing on this level have a physical form, or body, and a spiritual one. It is only our clouded vision that prevents us from seeing that this is so. And as we will discover, clouded vision can lead to apathy, depression, and various forms of paralysis and stagnation.

SPIRITUAL HEALING AS A LAST RESORT

When we delve further beneath the surface of Sign Two, Maryam presents more surprising lessons. The palace official in this episode has a son who is very ill and the court physician has been unable to help. Someone mentions that Yeshua is back in the Galilee. Why not try him—after all what is there to lose?

The official is used to telling others what to do and to getting what he wants. But he cannot command the help that his son and heir so desperately needs. He is in a difficult situation, for it was common knowledge that people like Yeshua did not meet with the approval of the tetrarch, Herod. He has to decide what matters most to him. It seems that this will mean moving out of his comfort zone to approach someone with whom he would never have dealings—a nomadic healer and friend of ordinary folk. But through swallowing his pride and admitting his vulnerability, by asking for help, he encounters the healing power of spiritual reality.

Today spiritual healing is still the therapy of last resort, and many hesitate to admit that they have tried it. For some people it is a matter of pride never to ask for any kind of help. Asking for help is not a sign of weakness. It could even be a turning point for the better in a person's life. The pride that keeps us aloof from others is a symptom of our belief in separation. True humility is not a lack of self-worth, but the recognition that we are part of each other.

TO SUM UP

DISTANT HEALING IS POSSIBLE
BECAUSE OF ONENESS

Many of Maryam's followers were living in dire straits and had joined the Jesus movement because it offered new hope, a new direction, and a new energy. In recognizing their own need for spiritual help, they had unconsciously heeded the call of the soul. The story of the palace official's son throws down a threefold challenge: Are you going to wait until life gets desperate before you heed the call of the soul? If that day comes, will you be too proud to reach out to others? Maryam's teachings offer a way to personal and world healing. This healing is perfectly possible because of Oneness, but will it be for you the path of last resort?

12
Sign Three

INERTIA
AND STAGNATION

Maryam's Story continues with Sign Three:

(John 5:1–19) After this there was a festival of the Jews, and Jesus went up to Jerusalem. Now in Jerusalem by the Sheep Gate there is a pool, called in Hebrew Beth-zatha, which has five porticoes. In these lay many invalids—blind, lame, and paralyzed. One man was there who had been ill for thirty-eight years. When Jesus saw him lying there and knew that he had been there a long time, he said to him, "Do you want to be made well?" The sick man answered him, "Sir, I have no one to put me into the pool when the water is stirred up; and while I am making my way, someone else steps down ahead of me." Jesus said to him, "Stand up, take your mat and walk." At once the man was made well, and he took up his mat and began to walk. Now that day was a Sabbath. So the Jews said to the man who had been cured, "It is the Sabbath; it is not lawful for you to carry your mat." But he answered them, "The man who made me well said to me, 'Take up your mat and walk.'" They asked

him, "Who is the man who said to you, 'Take it up and walk'?" Now
the man who had been healed did not know who it was, for Jesus had
disappeared in the crowd that was there. Later Jesus found him in
the temple and said to him, "See, you have been made well! Do not
sin anymore, so that nothing worse happens to you." The man went
away and told the Jews that it was Jesus who had made him well.
Therefore the Jews started persecuting Jesus, because he was doing
such things on the Sabbath. But Jesus answered them, "My Father is
still working, and I also am working." For this reason the Jews were
seeking all the more to kill him, because he was not only breaking the Sabbath, but was also calling God his own Father, thereby
making himself equal to God. Jesus said to them, "Very truly, I tell
you, the Son can do nothing on his own, but only what he sees the
Father doing; for whatever the Father does, the Son does likewise."

Yeshua's party makes a second pilgrimage to Jerusalem where they
arrive during Shabbat. They enter the city by the Sheep Gate where,
close by, there are two healing pools. The water from the higher pool
is periodically released into the lower pool, creating turbulence in its
waters. Yeshua motions them to visit the pool known as Bet Hisda
(Bethesda: "House of Mercy"). This pool is always crowded with the
sick and disabled. It is thought that when the waters begin to swirl,
divine power is available for healing. Yeshua goes into the pool house.
There is a stone bank around the pool where those seeking help sit or
lie. He walks among them and stops in front of a man lying on a worn-
out mat. He is crooked and bent with bitterness, and in the story we
know that he has been there for thirty-eight years. Yeshua asks him if he
wants to be healed. It is not a cruel question because of what happens.
The old man whines that he is paralyzed and cannot reach the water
when it swirls with the divine power. "By the time someone does help
me, and I manage to scramble down to the edge, the power has already
left the water. Every time it's the same. There's no hope for me." He
begins to sob.

Yeshua smiles at him and holds both his hands. "Then why are you here?" The man looks up. "In case it might happen." "So you think it might happen. Well, it won't happen if you have given up hope." Yeshua's voice changes. "Get up," he says quietly, but sternly. "You are healed." The man cannot believe it and begins to whine again, asking Yeshua who he is. Yeshua heaves the man to his feet. "Pick up your mat and get out of here." The man leans against the wall for support, but can feel the power returning to his limbs. He rolls up his filthy mat and staggers out without a backward glance. As Yeshua and some of his followers slip away, some of the disabled people cheer.

Meanwhile, a cluster of Judean people who had been looking after the sick in the pool house start murmuring. "Who was that, healing the sick on Shabbat?" they ask. As we know it is against Hebrew religious law to heal on the Sabbath, but Yeshua teaches that every day is holy—a teaching found among many indigenous peoples today. They run after the paralyzed man shouting: "Who was that, what happened?" The old man stops to catch his breath. "I don't know the man. He looked like a rabbi. He told me to get up and take my mat and walk out of there. He helped me up and I found I could do it. Even with these wasted old legs, I could walk again!" Instead of being thankful, they keep on muttering about breaking religious law and healing on the Sabbath.

Now the story takes us to the next scene in the temple. Yeshua is standing praying when the old man sidles up and taps him on the shoulder. Yeshua turns. "I see you are well again. Now let go of your envy and anger, especially your hatred, so that you don't become sick again. Next time it may be worse." The old man is stung by Yeshua's words. He feels that he was being told off. He finds the people that were muttering and points Yeshua out to them so that as Yeshua goes to leave the temple, he is surrounded by these men. They shout at him for breaking the Sabbath. Yeshua is quite calm. He talks to them in simple language. "My heavenly Father works every day, and so do I, his son. He has made every day holy." This really infuriates them.

Not only does he break the Sabbath, the blasphemer calls the Holy One his father and makes out he is the divine son. He deserves to be stoned to death!

A PARALYSIS
LASTING THIRTY-EIGHT YEARS

The paralyzed man had been living by the pool for thirty-eight years. The story is specific in mentioning this amount of time. Does that number of years mean anything to us? Maryam's followers would have known that the Jewish scriptures tell of how the Hebrews wandered through the desert for thirty-eight years. The story is speaking to us through this image of much wandering, and getting nowhere fast. First we go to celebrate the time of wandering and now, before we reach the Temple, we have to confront the reality of the wandering— it has been a time of paralysis. Have we been paralyzed, then? How can that be so?

LOOKING AT OUR OWN PARALYSIS

Before this Sign Story, we were suffering for a long time, wandering in the desert of ignorance of who we really are. Perhaps we embodied the fear that we could not change our state. The story of the paralyzed man helps us to identify the causes of suffering. We have been paralyzed by a range of strong and destructive feelings, but if we allow the soul to bring our wandering to an end, we will be healed of that paralysis. We can see a way forward and be ready to plan our future work. Though others may have tried to help us through this time, in the end our own soul has brought us to this place of healing. The healing has therefore included the toll on our mind and heart as well as our body. Fear may often induce a crippling paralysis, so can losing hope and feeling that there is nothing to live for.

Yeshua is telling us that our power comes from the sacred within us. We have to let go of all those feelings that were crippling us. The image of being born again was signaling that no one has to be a prisoner of his past. The water in the story has a twofold message: It is like the waters of the womb preparing us to be born again, but it is also a symbol of our emotions. There are negative emotions within us that we have the power to heal. These are the "waters" in which we need to be immersed. We cannot admire the man's determination to stay by the pool when he has only remained there because of his mental and emotional paralysis. Yeshua, as the soul, commands us to get up, walk away from paralysis, and release our mind from its state of stagnation and trust our heart. Here we will find our own House of Mercy and our own healing pool.

Much of the conditioning of the mind stands in the way of developing healing consciousness. It has been paralyzed up to the time of your decision to be born again. Now the mind is freed up so that sacred mind may be contacted. Paralysis in the form of inability to act or make decisions has prevented the expression of the sacred. We are ready to work with the effects of paralyzing fear and its roots in our own psyche.

You go to enter the capital again—your heart center. First you visit the pool to wash and refresh yourself. Then you encounter your own desert of inner paralysis. You have been waiting for a sign, for a leader, for someone to tell you what to do next. Yet, you are your own sign, your own leader. Arise! Get up and get moving or your mind will not function as it should.

RIPE AND UNRIPE

We may wonder why the story has to remind us about the truth of daily life. We already knew it, and yet we have been struggling to come to terms with what we knew. The story of the Third Sign suggests that a profound change of attitude is in order. A clue about how to do this lies in the fascinating language of Aramaic. Here, we find that all aspects of duality are a continuum, not pairs of opposites. For example, the words for good and evil do not reflect an abstract morality, instead they are about ripeness—what is ripe and what is not yet ripe; almost as if "evil" is in the process of becoming "good." It is simply a matter of time. We do not have to be paralyzed by the apparent negativity in the world. As Yeshua was showing all those in the healing pool, a change of attitude allows the negative to transform into the positive.

Each year Nature shows us how the patient process of maturation works. A story has it that one day a father took his son into the orchard. "I have something to show you." In his hand was a fat round orange. He held it out. "Smell its perfume. Would you say this fruit is sweet and ready to eat?" The boy took the orange and scratched the surface of the peel. Its perfume wafted up to him. "Yes, father. It is ready to eat." "Is it a good orange then?" "Yes, father. It is good." Then he pointed to the oranges on a branch nearby. They were still green with only a little orange showing. "Are they ready to eat, my son?" "Not yet, father, they aren't ripe yet." "Does that mean they are not good?" The boy wondered why he was being questioned in this way, and he did not want to give the wrong answer. "They are not bad, father, they have not ripened yet." "Then they will be good, is that it?" Then he saw the twinkle in his father's eye. "They are neither good nor bad, father. They are oranges. One day they will ripen. Then we will eat them and say they are good." The father stroked his son's head. "So it is with living things, my child. All living things are in the process of becoming ripe." "Even people?" The father laughed. "Especially people! Remember the oranges, when you think a person is bad or a person is good." That evening, as he lay in his bed, the boy smiled to himself and thought: so all things are in the process of becoming ripe—even me!

WHAT REALITY DO WE SEE?

It is still early in our pilgrimage story, but we are being reminded that it is important to be aware of how we are seeing. We tend to look at something from a limited, preconditioned point of view. This means that we only half see what is there. However, when we become a fully realized person, we see with the eye of the heart, and we see things as they are. Then life is neither good nor evil, it just is. We need to trust our own deep awareness.

The reality that we perceive is partial and our perception is always through the filter of our individual conditioning. Everyone's filter is unique so that each of us has a unique perception of reality. We tend to ignore the reality that our unique perception has a spiritual foundation and origin. Thus we tend to grasp for what is unreal, cling to what is unreal, and depend on what is unreal as we identify with whom we *think* we are. As if we sense that reality might be different somewhere else, we try to escape to another place of unreality, only to find that we meet ourselves there.

The suffering person shrinks from learning to simply be. Any thoughts, emotions, anxieties, and fears—which upset our sense of harmony—prevent the healthy state. So we need to allow them to simply be there without focusing on them and giving them attention. Without our undivided attention, they will slowly fade. We do not have to fear either the causes or the symptoms of disharmony. We can learn to choose. A way to choose is to practice letting go.

We can make the most of every experience. This means not agonizing over making a decision, about whether it is right or wrong, either before, during, or after. We will find out by experience and experience is life. Every experience has possibilities. We do not need to be defensive about how we live, how we look, or how we appear to others. We need to take risks, but in a state of doubt it is best not to act until the mind is clear. Let go into the flow of life and discover the joy of being in this living flow.

Expressing gratitude lets the energy flow and completes the circle of energy. Ingratitude or non-expression acts as a block to the flow. You can choose what to do.

ACCEPTING CHANGE

It may also be difficult to grasp that we each choose what we want to experience until we realize the all-powerful divine aspect of ourselves. Some things that happen to us may seem like difficult challenges: perhaps a lesson about attachment to someone or some thing, perhaps the lesson of letting go, perhaps the lesson of learning to give and receive. Whatever the reason, every challenge brings us closer to an understanding and realization of who we really are. When things happen that we do not like, we tend to fight with life rather than accept things as they are presented to us. When something changes, by overlooking the greater picture, we fail to see the fresh challenges that each moment gives us as opportunities. We need to learn to let go of trying to control life and let our soul self live through us. This is the lesson the paralyzed man had to learn.

The healing way is about accepting change because we change, people change, situations change, everything is changing at every moment. Nothing stays the same. Perhaps we find this inevitable life process stressful, until one day we realize that it is our reactions that are creating stress. When we fight life, we are actually fighting ourselves, trying to control things so that they fulfill our wants and desires. But we do have control over our choices.

TAKE CARE OF YOURSELF

As it is getting near time to travel north to the next Sign, we can rest assured that we will be protected and shown where to go. At the same time, we are being warned about vigilance and about whom to trust. We are all one, but our soul lives here—on the Earth—in the world of opposites. It is our destiny to express the beauty of the divine, but this does not mean that we do not take good care of ourselves. In the world it is natural for the complete opposite of what we consider good to be present.

CHANGE YOUR MIND-SET
BY PAYING ATTENTION

Other people, other beings, and situations act as mirrors for us, reflecting to us who we are. When we pay attention to someone, some thing, or some situation, our awareness grows. This leads to greater understanding and new insights. As consciousness expands, our awareness is that the life we first thought of in terms of duality is, in fact, a unity. Here in the physical universe, here on planet Earth, duality is the norm and it's okay. By paying attention in this way, we add our creative energy to the process of life, to being Life.

Maryam is helping us realize that there are no accidents and no coincidences. Each life is full of signs and symbols and they are there to be intuited as a form of play. If we are not paying attention, we will miss most of the signs and symbols that life is presenting to us. Even if the conditioned and fragmented mind cannot grasp this, we simply need to be aware of its limitations—it only knows what it *already* knows and our previous reactions to experience will condition how the mind will present our perceptions to us.

TO SUM UP

SEPARATION FROM THE SOURCE
IS THE ROOT OF FEAR

The universe is multidimensional, with many levels of being. Each of us is simultaneously living in many dimensions and, happily, the mind presents us with the level that we can best understand. This tends to be that part of the physical world that we can perceive and not the many invisible levels that envelop it. This impression of the world is what the mind has created from what little it already knows.

You don't need to get distracted by what may or may not be illusory, however. Instead, look out for signs that your awareness is growing: that paying attention is beginning to become a way of being, that all life is sacred. When you find less violence and aggression appearing in your thoughts, words, and actions, you are beginning to cultivate a center of peace and stillness within yourself.

Toward the end of this episode about the healing pool, Maryam cautions us to remain alert. Nevertheless, we do not need to fear what we sense as darkness, for darkness is not the opposite of light, but the absence of light. When there is no separation from the Source, there can be nothing to fear. When we sense a lack of something, the light of heart perception would tell us that there is always enough of what we need.

13

Sign Four

THERE IS ALWAYS ENOUGH

Maryam's Story again takes on a dreamlike quality, for it seems that a year has passed as we are drawing near Passover time once more. We are back in Yeshua's own country, away from the Judean capital, on the far side of the great expanse of Lake Kinneret (the Sea of Galilee).

(John 6:1–15) After this Jesus went to the other side of the Sea of Galilee, also called the Sea of Tiberias. A large crowd kept following him, because they saw the signs that he was doing for the sick. Jesus went up the mountain and sat down there with his disciples. Now the Passover, the festival of the Jews, was near. When he looked up and saw a large crowd coming toward him, Jesus said to Philip, "Where are we to buy bread for these people to eat?" He said this to test him, for he himself knew what he was going to do. Philip answered him, "Six months' wages would not buy enough bread for each of them to get a little." One of his disciples, Andrew, Simon Peter's brother, said to him, "There is a boy here who has five barley loaves and two fish. But what are they among so many people?" Jesus said, "Make the people sit down." Now there was a great deal of grass in the place; so they sat down, about five thousand in all. Then Jesus took the loaves, and when he had given thanks, he distributed them to those who were seated; so also the fish, as much as they wanted. When they were satisfied, he told his disciples, "Gather up the fragments left over, so that nothing may be lost." So they gathered them up, and from the fragments of the five barley loaves, left by those who had eaten, they filled twelve baskets. When the people saw the sign that he had done, they began to say, "This is indeed the prophet who is to come into the world." When Jesus realized that they were about to come and take him by force to make him king, he withdrew again to the mountain by himself.

Hemmed in by people who all want something, Yeshua tries to escape from the crowds who have heard about his healing. So the group asks some fishermen to take them across to the eastern side of Kinneret. There, they climb the hillside and stop to rest. As they look around, they see that a huge crowd has still managed to follow them. Philip was ready to make a note of Yeshua's words to the followers, but Yeshua asks him how they are going to feed the people. Philip says that they could not afford to buy food for such a multitude. Yeshua laughs and waves his arm. "There is no food up here anyway."

Just then, Andrew appears. With him is a boy holding a travel bag. He tips the bag onto the grass and out falls a cloth inside which are a few flat breads and some dried fish. Andrew asks how they think they can feed the people with this paltry amount of food. Yeshua looks across to the crowd and sees a family smiling at him. They have sent the boy over with the food. Yeshua waves to them and the followers shout their thanks. Like any pious Jew, Yeshua spreads out the piece of cloth on which to place the food, holds his hands over the food and offers up thanks and a blessing. Then he pulls off a piece of bread and a tiny piece of fish and passes round the cloth with the rest of the food. In this way, each of the followers has a morsel of food. The family watches. Slowly, other families have followed their example and done the same, everyone is sharing something.

Yeshua knows that the people have not come to eat but to hear what he has to say and to ask for favors such as healing. It is unusual for people to leave any food, apart from crumbs of bread or fish bones, on the ground. Nevertheless, instead of leaving the crumbs of food for the birds, Yeshua asks the followers to gather them up. It is the custom to pack food for traveling in little baskets made of woven palm leaves. A number of these are passed round to gather up the crumbs. Sometimes leftover bread is put in soup, a custom still common to countries all around the Mediterranean.

Many in the crowd come over and look at the twelve baskets. They are saying things like: "The prophet sets a good example for us. He shares whatever he has, just as we have been taught." Others are saying: "He is the messiah we've been waiting for. He'll get rid of the Roman oppressors." To set such an example apparently makes him the expected messiah. These remarks are strange since it is the custom for people to share what they have. They do not seem to have gotten the message that he was not the messiah they wanted, in fact he wasn't anyone's messiah, and his teaching was that every person has a messiah within them. Yeshua and his group pack their things and climb higher, leaving the crowd behind.

THE CHALLENGE TO CLIMB HIGHER

Keep in touch with your feelings, for they are playing a prominent role in the Story. In the fourth Sign story, the Rabbi encourages his followers to climb away from the body of water, only to confront what appeared to be another difficulty. On facing it the difficulty fades into nothing. There was nothing to overcome. They leave that place and climb even higher.

Perhaps for Maryam this story reminds her of the days of travel with the Rabbi—eating together, talking together, simply being together—

that have since become a painful memory. The image of the crowd also reminds her of the challenge before her to go back to them and carry on with the work that she and Yeshua had begun together.

We hear echoes of the paralysis of the previous dream in the panic of the followers. First the wariness of large crowds—a natural reaction when any sign of a crowd makes both Roman and Hebrew officials edgy. Second, they worry that there won't be enough to feed the crowd. Yet into the story comes the embodiment of courage and bravery, Andreas. Now we can look at the great lesson described by Maryam as Yeshua leads the group up the hillside, away from the banks of the vast lake, to a higher place where they could rest and refresh themselves.

When we move away from the domination of our anxieties, and the concerns of the mind, to the place of the heart, by "climbing higher," we allow soul to guide us and things change, just as we found in the dream stories of the previous three Signs.

When love takes over, fear fades away. Where fear always takes the despondent stance and sees lack and scarcity, love tells us there is always enough. This is the symbol of the baskets of crumbs.

THE MEANING OF THE LOAVES AND FISHES AND THE TWELVE BASKETS

Maryam's teaching takes us further as the prophet shows the people that there is always enough *love* to go round. In Aramaic, the bread in the story, *lakhma,* is a perfect symbol for *rakhma,* "love." Both words are based on KhM, an ancient Semitic root signifying both warmth and "womb" or a place of nurture and safety, a root that also appears in the Hebrew word for wisdom: khokhmah. To nourish the body we eat bread, but the greatest nourishment is love. Hence, Yeshua asks us to collect up the crumbs, and we find that there was more than enough. This is how it is with love: don't hesitate to share it, to give it out because there is always more than enough.

When Maryam mentions specific numbers, she is using them to

expand the meaning of the signs: five loaves and two fishes. Her listeners would have picked up on the linguistic link between bread, universal love, and the love of a mother. They would have also heard deep meaning in the word *nunah,* "fish," for the letter *nun* symbolizes one who is there to serve the people, rather than save them. The natural medium for the fish is water, but it is forced to reveal itself on dry land. This parallels the life of the holy person who has to reveal who they are in order to teach and serve the people.

The loaves are five symbols of nurturing love. For Maryam's Jewish audience, these might well be the five books of Moses: the Torah. These are accompanied by the equally nourishing two fishes or two "messiahs." Again, her listeners might well have put two and two together and seen the two fish as Yeshua and Maryam. They have not come to supplant the Torah but to make it alive and relevant to new and turbulent times. Plunging deeper we recall that Maryam's name begins and ends with *mem,* "water." She embodies the feminine as he embodies the masculine. Together they form the unity of the two energy streams. Finally, the number of loaves and fishes adds up to seven: the sacred number of completion.

The number twelve has traveled with the Jews since they became an ancient people. The first image that would probably come to the minds of Maryam's followers would be the twelve tribes of Israel. This brings us again to the figure of Jacob and all that he represents in the Story, for his twelve sons are said to have given rise to the twelve tribes. Some would also have known that the twelve tribes symbolize the twelve senses or means by which the soul encounters the physical realm. These twelve senses also connect us with the spiritual realm and help us to reach healing consciousness.

LOVE ALWAYS PROVIDES

Having looked at some of the inner meanings of the Sign Four episode, we are always counseled to keep it simple. We are not Pharisees or

Sadducees who thought that attention to religious and academic detail
made them righteous people. We are learning about love, that the deepest and most powerful love is unconditional and unlimited, like the
love of a messiah. We each have an inner messiah, the soul, whose love
is always unconditional and unlimited. Maryam is teaching that since
the universe *is* the Source, it follows that the universe *is* love. Thus the
universe will always provide what is needed. But, the story reminds us,
mind thinks there is only so much of anything. This is why we scrabble
around as if there will never be enough—of bread, of belongings, of
friends, of safety, of pleasure, of money, of anything.

Many of the men in the Yeshua and Maryam movement had great
difficulty with his love. Some complained that he loved everyone, as if
his love for them was therefore worthless, as if there were some limit to
love. Others complained that he loved Maryam more than them (Gospel
of Philip), as if that made them inferior to her. Yeshua and Maryam
came together to teach together, to show the world something greater
than any words—there is always enough of everything, especially love.
How could he not show his love for her, his twin soul? They knew it,
but they just could not bear that he loved a special woman. They were
still learning about love.

STAY WITH THE HEART

Again, at the close of the story, we are warned to be prepared. Some will
be grateful whenever the presence of the Holy One is demonstrated,
but others will miss the point and look to their own need for a leader,
or someone to blame, rather than take responsibility for their own
lives. The Hebrew people had been crying out to be free, and some of
Yeshua's followers wanted him to drive out the Romans and bring them
freedom from oppression. But he taught that to be truly free, we have
to take responsibility for ourselves. He was hated for that. So how then
will we behave?

Maryam counsels us to stay with our heart, say what we have to say, understand what we have to understand, experience what we have to experience. Then, we can move to the higher ground of the spirit, staying with our understanding and experience of the One, living in the dwelling place of our soul. Though we are the embodiment of the sacred, we may find it hard to accept that we have everything we need within us. But we are all aspects of the One, and the One is expressing life through us. An ant is God being an ant, a flower is God being a flower, and a human being is God being a human being. This is hinted at by the Old Testament shaman Iyov (Job) where he suggests that if we ask them, the animals, birds, plants, and fish can teach us about God (Job 12).

WALKING THE PATH OF THE HEART

It takes discipline, strength, and courage to accept who we are. We may find it easier to avoid looking closely at ourselves because we have unconsciously accepted the images and stereotypes created by our family, society, religion, and culture. It is as if we have forgotten how to honor our unique potential, our particular strengths and weaknesses, fearing the emergence of the deep part of ourselves that we keep hidden from each other. But the dark and the light live together in the heart.

A healer is someone who walks the path of the heart, understanding and accepting her own true nature. The path of the heart is lived by consciously creating our reality. Once the heart is encouraged to guide us, the conditioned mind is able to be of service instead of dominating our reactions to life.

Taking up the path of the heart does not mean taking up asceticism. The path of the heart takes us deep into life—our own life, the life of others, the life of the Earth and the Earth family. For the heart, where the soul dwells, encourages a total giving out of resources and, above all, a total giving out of love, without attaching any conditions. This way of being is very evident in all the gospels where Yeshua gives everything that he has to give—without counting the cost—in an extravagant, almost reckless giving. Our own circumstances often suggest that we should hold on to what we have, that to share a certain resource would be folly. Yet this is exactly the moment to follow the path of the heart, for when we worry about resources, we have forgotten from where they came and what they really are.

Just now people in the more affluent parts of the world are presented with this challenge as others who have far less than we do arrive at our gates, asking for help, succor, and safety.

THE HEART SPACE

I mentioned in chapter 1 how, as a very young child, I was able to find a place of warm retreat within myself that I call the "Heart Space." This is the "place" at the core of Magdalene spirituality. We all need that place of retreat, safety, warmth, and comfort where endless love is generated. It exists, and it is reachable. Above all it is a place of strength. But it is worth remembering that our upbringing and conditioning may have dimmed our awareness of it and therefore its accessibility. Even though it is always there, it is possible to lose touch with the childhood Heart Space. As the personality gradually takes control and is forced to interact with the society and culture in which it finds itself, we tend to move farther and farther away from the Heart Space, the place of spiritual retreat. Having a religious upbringing may not necessarily help, for many religions have hijacked the childhood Heart Space and robbed us of it. Our spiritual consciousness has been taken away, put outside, somewhere else, or even lodged in some other person, anywhere but in our own heart.

This is very important for anyone brought up within a religion that says you are not God. Without positive reinforcement of the Heart Space, by the time young people reach adolescence, they have lost this safe retreat and any consciousness or memory of it. In today's secular society, not only is there no God inside you, there is no God outside you either. So the personality tries to fill the void. It seeks once again to be a god by becoming a celebrity, a star, or by achieving fame or notoriety of some kind. Other ways of compensating for the lost Heart Space take the many forms of materialism, mind-numbing activities, and a whole range of addictive behaviors.

The Heart Space is not simply a place to hide. It is somewhere to go when life's negativity is too great to bear, yes, but by going there we are nurtured because it reconnects us with our own sacred reality. I can see that this was why Maryam's first signal to me in the cave, a lifetime after the gift of the beach vision, was via the heart. My attention was strongly drawn to my physical heart, and then her presence and message lifted me to the subtle and spiritual levels of the heart energy center, situated in the middle of the chest. She found the perfect way to strongly focus me there.

The guidance of this great feminine shaman-prophet and master teacher is to begin in the heart, the place of the soul. Listen to the voice in your heart. Then note how your mind immediately has a problem—there is nothing in the mind's memory bank with which to compare the soul voic; therefore, it does not compute. But the mind *does* have access to all kinds of doubts and negative waves, so it offers up those thoughts for your consideration. This is when I recall Maryam's assurance: "You can call on me any time to help you." In other words we can allow her to help us access the sacred soul and its voice. She is there in the Heart Space.

TO SUM UP

THE CHOICE OF MIND OR HEART OR PERHAPS BOTH

The heart is the driving force behind Maryam's program for personal transformation because the heart center is the place of the soul.

The impasse that everyone reaches is the choice between the quiet guidance of the heart and the louder insistence of the mind. In Sign Four some of the followers became angry or afraid of the crowd that had collected at a time when they needed a rest and a meal break. With hardly enough for themselves, their fearful thoughts were about how to feed that quantity of people. They had lost faith in the power of love and could not believe that the universe will provide. Later writers described "the feeding of the five thousand" as a miracle, while many contemporary writers have suggested the simple explanation to which I have deliberately hinted—that the crowd sees Yeshua and his followers sharing what they have and they do the same—for very few people traveled without some sustenance for their trip and sharing was part of the Semitic tradition of hospitality and respect for strangers.

A further explanation needs to be taken on board, namely that the miracles ascribed to Yeshua would have been possible. When a person is totally aligned with the Source—as Yeshua and Maryam were—the seemingly miraculous always occurs *because* such alignment makes them conduits for all that is. They are totally aligned spiritually and, therefore, energetically.

Whatever explanation we choose, in Maryam's transformation Story, the Sign points away from debate to the deeper message. This time it points to the healing consciousness that there is always enough. To be truly free, we will have to listen more carefully to the voice of the heart. Until this becomes habitual practice, our mind will react to situations where the lack of something seems to be apparent, encouraging us to move into fear mode. Our emotions will tell us about these reactions, and this is where Maryam takes us in Sign Five.

14

Sign Five

THE SEA OF EMOTIONS

Jesus Walks on Water • Revealing the I AM •
Living in Shacks • More Rumbles in the Temple

The symbol of water, occurring once again, is significant and powerful, an understanding going back to the wisdom of the ancients. Our bodies, we know, are made mainly of liquids, therefore, of water. Water, the ancients taught, tells us about human emotions.

JESUS WALKS ON WATER

Maryam's Teaching Story continues,

(John 6:16–21) When evening came, his disciples went down to the sea, got into a boat, and started across the sea to Capernaum. It was now dark, and Jesus had not yet come to them. The sea became rough because a strong wind was blowing. When they had rowed about three or four miles, they saw Jesus walking on the sea and coming near the boat, and they were terrified. But he said to them, "It is I; do not be afraid." Then they wanted to take him into the boat, and immediately the boat reached the land toward which they were going.

The sea is the sum of waters, the source of clouds and rain. It may be so calm that we can see the beautiful image of the moon on its surface. But who does not fear to be out at sea when a storm rages and the heaving waves rise up to great heights? Thus it is with our emotions. And so we find our pilgrimage Story talking again about being near water. As we face that great lake, which has moods as intense as any in the Mediterranean, will we find that we have absorbed the message of the healing pool?

We are still in the hills above Lake Kinneret (the Sea of Galilee). Yeshua and Maryam spend the afternoon talking to the group. When Maryam speaks, some of the men are annoyed and embarrassed. They get up to go to the shore. They untie a boat and intend to sail back the way they came, to Capernaum where Yeshua and Maryam went after the wedding ceremony. But they have left some of the group, and, as if their mood has affected the weather, a cloud appears over the hill and a strong wind moves the cloud so that it covers the great lake. It grows dark and a storm comes up. The waters reflect the black sky. The waves grow higher and begin to rock the boat. The men are afraid and wish they had waited for the rest of the group to join them. Yeshua can see they are in trouble and so he walks over the water to the boat. This makes them even more afraid. They think: How can he do this? He must be a spirit of some kind. Yeshua calls out to them to remain calm in their hearts, but they are still afraid. This tells us that, unlike Maryam, they are unaware of his total alignment with the Source. It also tells us that it is she who was best qualified to lead the new Galilean spiritual movement after Yeshua's death.

WHO WILL STAY THE COURSE
AND WHO WILL LEAVE?

In an echo of the way fear can stop us moving forward, as in Sign Three, Maryam sees some of the followers going back. It may be easier to do this when the going gets tough, but Maryam does not join the retreating followers, she simply shows herself the possibility. She stays with her heart's guidance and watches as she sees the outcome of losing courage and regressing. Even at the point of falling overboard and drowning, the Divine can come to the rescue in what seems a miraculous way. Life is full of such small miracles. We may feel ashamed of our lapses, which are only human, but the heart does not judge and does not give up on us.

In dream healing, when we think of water, especially a lake or the sea, we think of the dreamer's emotions. Listening to their negative emotions, those who will not follow Maryam, the woman teacher, want to leave. When they looked at her as the beautiful woman that she was, perhaps some of the male disciples also feared their own desires and emotions, which were like a powerful storm or a turbulent sea in which they might drown. But there is a warning against their leaving. This is not her wish for them as a kind of punishment, but a knowing on her part that they will fall into danger if they leave her. They do not listen to their heart's voice, but leave in ignorance, taking their ignorance with them, leaving both Maryam and Yeshua.

At the time of Maryam's teaching, Yeshua had been executed by the Roman occupiers of Palestine. This would have made listening to a series of stories about him a very painful experience for many of their followers. Thus the narrative of Sign Five would have been a poignant reminder of what actually happened: the departure of some of the male disciples.

THE NEED TO BE IN CONTROL

In Maryam's Teaching Story Yeshua's followers react with fear when they realize that they cannot control the effects of Nature. Fear-based emotions like these are the result of our mind's reactions to a situation. If we make choices based on such reactions, we may think we are in control, but we are actually being controlled by our emotional reactions. The energetic effect is that we cannot control another person or another situation. The way to bring about control is to bring about inner change and acceptance. Then, ironically, we find that we have no need to control anyone or any situation since we are part of the flow of life, not trying to impede the flow or divert its course. This is the meaning of walking on water and calming the storm— two dramatic metaphors for not being intimidated by our emotional reactions.

Fear is the opposite of love; it undermines the loving response. Yet love always has the answer. So now your heart is challenged in another way: the personal threat from natural forces. Being authentic is the challenge. This is the love for one's inner being, which is then given out to honor others by offering them your truth. Now is the time to "walk your talk." Can you really live as if all dualities are one? You and the water are one. You and the storm are one. You can calm your emotions. You can overcome all storms. The soul in the heart center tells you to love not fear. You can be you.

YOU ARE IN CHARGE OF YOUR JOURNEY

The Signs point to a path of transformation, but the journey is your journey and how you decide to travel it is your choice. As you go deeper and your consciousness expands, the path may seem to become more difficult and suddenly stormier. Here, the heart and the conditioned mind confront each other. In Sign Four we may have resolved to follow the path of the heart. We feel uplifted, until our resolve sets off the survival alarm bells of the mind. Now it seems we must choose one over the other or even give up. But Sign Five shows that if you stay with your path, the waters of your stormy emotions can be overcome, and your inner turmoil can be calmed. At this point you discover how vitally important it is to be prepared for the journey, and how careful and thorough your own preparations were. Thus there was the essential time in the Wilderness before you engaged with Sign One. If you feel it necessary, you could pause here to reassess your time in the Wilderness.

NATURE IS NOT TO BE FEARED

Nature always reveals the presence of the sacred. For Maryam this would mean the presence of I AM. We may wonder whether her Story is asking us to reflect on this or whether the tossing waves and the dark clouds reflect our own negative feelings. One of the many teachings of Sign Five is that Nature is not to be feared but respected, not to be overcome but honored. Natural law teaches that if we sow fear we reap the consequences of fear; if we sow love we reap the consequences of love. Even so, Yeshua, the compassionate, shows his terrified followers—in the most dramatic way—that they have nothing to fear. He walks on the water and calms the storm. Similar events have been reported with other teachers of the Hebrews and neighboring lands. But in Maryam's Story we are not being asked to believe in Yeshua, the soul, because he can work wonders, for personal transformation requires more than blind faith or unquestioning belief. As with all the other seemingly miraculous happenings in the Teaching Story, the miracles are signs pointing to the real message—Yeshua is not afraid of the storm or the sea because he is conscious of being one with them. He is aligned with the source of all storms and seas.

TO SUM UP

THE REAL MIRACLE

Alignment of consciousness with Oneness shows us that it is quite possible to put ourselves above our emotions, to travel across their surface. And it is possible to weather the storms and turmoil that life has brought us. Fear is the enemy of these possibilities—the same fear that paralyzed the person back at the healing pool, the same fear that prevents people from contacting their inner truth, the same fear of taking responsibility for their own lives and their own destiny. The Signs of walking on water and calming a storm point to the real miracle: that we can "walk on water" and be above the demands of negative emotions. Even when emotions are turbulent, it is possible to "calm the storm." We need to remember these lessons in the future when we will need their guidance.

REVEALING THE I AM

As we saw in the episodes "Being Born Again," and "The Woman at the Well," in chapter 10 we come to another "space" between the Signs. In Maryam's teachings these interludes are living spaces, not mere gaps in the Story. They each have the potential to reveal further facets of Maryam's main teaching theme: the removal of our clouded vision. In so doing they add extra strength and integrity to the wisdom of the Seven Signs. Even though the spaces between and the stories themselves are one continuous process, a second function of the interludes is their energetic potential to provide space for rest, healing, and renewal. This potential is most fully realized in your heart center.

Most healing needs time and space for the process. Each Sign story includes a range of elements and forces and each, in turn, generates new forces. We need time and space to absorb these forces and for them to permeate those levels of our being at which healing is required. Thus the space between the stories is alive with creative potential. And, equally, the time and space where new consciousness will develop depends on each person and her circumstances. There lies the healer's skill and the healer's calling.

So we turn to the space between our own dreams to meditate on the forces released through the drama of our nocturnal life. Perhaps we have struggled to accept what has happened to us in life and struggled to understand and take responsibility for our feelings, but this is essential if we are to discover who we really are and our life's purpose. Give thanks if you can see that Maryam's dream Story is showing you how to do this, for once you have reached this stage of the Seven Signs Story, you are ready to embrace a deeper understanding of your identity as a human being. With this next interlude Maryam retells one of Yeshua's most controversial teachings. A number of scholars consider it to be deliberately mistranslated, as is the case with many of Yeshua's contentious doctrines.

(John 6:22–33) The next day the crowd that had stayed on the other side of the sea saw that there had been only one boat there. They also saw that Jesus had not got into the boat with his disciples, but that his disciples had gone away alone. Then some boats from Tiberias came near the place where they had eaten the bread after the Lord had given thanks. So when the crowd saw that neither Jesus nor his disciples were there, they themselves got into the boats and went to Capernaum looking for Jesus. When they found him on the other side of the sea, they said to him, "Rabbi, when did you come here?" Jesus answered them, "Very truly, I tell you, you are looking for me, not because you saw signs, but because you ate your fill of the loaves. Do not work for the food that perishes, but for the food that endures for eternal life, which the Son of Man will give you. For it is on him that God the Father has set his seal." Then they said to him, "What must we do to perform the works of God?" Jesus answered them, "This is the work of God, that you believe in him whom he has sent." So they said to him, "What sign are you going to give us then, so that we may see it and believe you? What work are you performing? Our ancestors ate the manna in the wilderness; as it is written, 'He gave them bread from heaven to eat.'" Then Jesus said to them, "Very truly, I tell you, it was not Moses who gave you the bread from heaven, but it is my Father who gives you the true bread from heaven. For the bread of God is that which comes down from heaven and gives life to the world." They said to him, "Sir, give us this bread always." Jesus said to them, "I am the bread of life . . ."

As in a dream sequence, somehow the rest of the followers have landed on the far shore. The boat with the men on board arrives. They apologize for leaving but they don't look at Maryam. She can feel their shame. They do not seem surprised that the followers have arrived before them. It was the worst thing they could have done, for the crowd was waiting for them, waiting to mob Yeshua again. They went backward, back to the crowds they sought to avoid.

The crowd is baffled by Yeshua's appearance, though it is he they have been waiting for. Yeshua chides them and says that they only want him because he can do wondrous things for them, not because they want the presence of the Holy One. He speaks to the followers in a quiet voice, but they can hear him clearly. His words make some in the crowd angry. Yeshua climbs onto a large boulder and shouts: "You want me because you had enough to eat up there, even though you saw what really happened. If I have any power at all it comes from the Holy One, not me. I am an ordinary person like you." "How can we get the power then?" they shout. "Moshe led our ancestors out of Egypt across the desert. There was always enough bread then—are you Moshe?" There is derisive laughter as the mood of the crowd is turning. They wait for Yeshua's answer thinking that they have made a fool of him.

He waits for them to grow quiet, for he is about to tell them something that many will find hard to swallow. "It was not Moshe—may his name be blessed—who gave our ancestors the bread. It was I AM. Holy Oneness, the I AM, gives you bread now. More than this, I AM gives you food for your souls." "All right then," they shout back, "give us some of that soul bread. Let's see it." Many begin laughing again. Yeshua is unafraid. He repeats: "I AM is the bread of life. I AM is here now, in the bread, in you and in me." Many in the crowd are furious. They think he is quoting from the scriptures to justify himself. Others mishear and think he is blaspheming by saying he is the Holy One. Yet, if we look carefully, we can see a few beautiful faces in the crowd who understand what he has said. But we know that there are some, in their fear and hatred, who want to kill him. Maryam always knew this and had that feeling many times.

Finally, Maryam takes us back to the bread of life and the sacred womb that we encountered in Sign Four as she refers again to a story that is very dear to her. In chapter 8 she guided us to the Hebrew scripture called Shemot (Exodus) to the story of how the name for the deepest concept of the Divine was revealed to the shaman-prophet Moses as I AM.

Later religious authorities seem to prefer other names, but Yeshua encouraged his followers to use I AM as another word for Sacred Oneness, the Source. Even so, he knew that the people found it difficult to relate to the seemingly abstract I AM so he would often talk in a more personal way about Abba, their spiritual parent, that he was a son of the Father (in Hebrew *bar Abba,* in Greek *Barabbas*).

THE I AM IS LIFE ITSELF

At the beginning of Maryam's teachings (chapter 7), in her opening scene someone is singing about how divine energy became a soul and took on human flesh and then spoke as the I AM Presence, the same I AM that had been speaking throughout the centuries before Yeshua, as it did to Moses, for example. Throughout the Gospel of Signs, therefore, whenever Yeshua speaks, he speaks as this eternal I AM and not simply as the Jewish Yeshua. This deeper understanding of the Gospel reveals an emphasis on something much larger, more universal, and more profoundly relevant than a single human incarnation in Palestine. In this light we realize that the I AM statements of Yeshua are the expressive manifestation of the Source speaking, the same manifestation that was expressing itself before Yeshua and will continue to act through All That Is throughout time. Obviously the I AM is not exclusive to any religion, or to any group of people, rather it totally includes all beings.

Maryam describes how Yeshua once said to the group: "Think how wonderful that long ago someone recorded Moshe's conversation with

Holy Oneness where he discovers a great secret." "What is that secret?" they asked. "Why," he laughed, "the secret is that every time you think or say 'I am' you are discovering who you truly are. You are I AM. Each of us is I AM!" They were astounded. Could it be so? Yeshua saw their amazement. "Think further," he said. "The I AM said: 'I will be what I will be.' I AM is the Creation—what is happening right now, what has been happening and what is going to happen. I AM is life itself." Imagine some of the followers looking at each other, seeking reassurance, trying to take in his message that each of them was a facet of the One, that every life was therefore sacred and that this was the eternal truth of being.

THE BREAD OF LIFE

Yeshua would have spoken in Aramaic saying: *Ena-enah lakhmah d'khaye,* "I AM is the bread of life." Repeat the phrase, feeling how the sound "ah" resonates in your heart center. People in the crowd were brought up with the story of Moses, and Yeshua seized the opportunity to remind them about the I AM. Perhaps he had in fact cleverly guided them there with his talk of bread.

Traditionally, just as wine was a symbol for wisdom, bread was a symbol of understanding—Blake's "bread of sweet thought." Yeshua offered people a fresh understanding of the food that we all hunger for, the "food" he talked about during the episode in Samaria. By inserting this in her Teaching Story, Maryam, too, offers us a new understanding about spiritual nourishment.

THE PRICE OF KEEPING
THE I AM SEPARATE

Just quietly saying "I am" to ourselves can help us remember who we are. In conversation every one of us says "I am . . ." but it does not strike us that we are constantly describing ourselves as Sacred Unity. This is because throughout history organized religion has sought to maintain, and indeed increase, its power by keeping I AM separate from us. I AM is up there, out of sight, anywhere but not within each of us. Life controlled by religion maintained this separation by introducing intermediaries between us and Sacred Unity. Religious life could ensure our eventual reconnection with the sacred, after death, as long as we adhered to its doctrines and dogmas during life. The devastating reality is that this has blinded us to the true nature of ourselves and the sacred nature of the world and life itself.

This identifies the core problem that the Church later had with the revolutionary teachings of the Galilean spiritual master, Yeshua, who expended his life energies proclaiming that the "kingdom" (the experience and reality of I AM/Oneness) is within us. To enter this state of consciousness, we must go within. The alternative is to go without. Perhaps the church shrewdly understood human psychology when it took away the I AM Presence from each heart and put it "up there." At that time the majority of society demonstrated that it did not want to take responsibility for its spiritual well-being. People would much rather be led and then blame the leader when things went wrong. They would much rather follow a savior than realize that "salvation" was in their own hands. There is plenty of evidence to suggest that this thinking still prevails in societies all over the world. But there is even greater evidence of a universal awakening as we wake up to the truth of our own spiritual identity, the interrelatedness of all life, the sacredness of life, and the love for our planet and all of nature.

With the introduction of the concept of savior, and responsibility in the hands of God or his representatives, people needed a set of commandments to keep them in line. But, as history shows, we cannot keep them when awareness of I AM is not in our hearts. Having a set of moral rules has not prevented any religious culture from breaking them, and their members will quote scripture to justify it. This means there can be no Oneness. It means that we can hurt others because we are not one with them. It means we can make war on, kill, steal from, betray, abuse, and persecute others because we are not one with them. It means we can and should exploit nature as well as other people. It means we have arrived at the present catastrophic dilemmas, many of them in the name of the Divine.

If this is what has happened because of our disconnection from the sacred, then the recovery of the I AM Presence in every heart is the way forward. With the teachings of the Seven Signs, Maryam has created the energetic structure by which we can achieve this goal.

FINDING YOUR IDENTITY

There may come a time on the path where you have to let go of the familial and social structures and organizations that provide you with your assumed identity. You may feel a new sense of freedom that you have moved beyond these earlier conditions and restrictions. But if in the process you have forgotten the I AM within, the thought may hit: If I have no real connection with all that previously gave me my identity as a person and a member of society, then who am I? All we know is what we are not. We do not yet know who we truly are, and the answers we seek are only to be found within.

Fears arise when we cannot find our answer or cannot hear the answer because we are just not that aware. We may go on to ask ourselves: What if I am on the wrong track anyway and there is no answer? What if this stuff is just to make me join some religion or even a cult? And so the fear-based messages of the mind pour into the solar plexus center, and our stomach lurches with our sense of isolation and loneliness. These emotions are only a state of mind. In reality, at every moment, we are connected to the Source, to Nature and the whole of the cosmos, and to our own souls, because we *are* the Godsource, we *are* I AM. This connection and this truth are experienced through love.

In a fearful state we experience disconnection and separation; there seems no way that we could possibly be the Source. We have the evidence of our own senses that the idea is preposterous. However, if we take the route of such negative thoughts, which can only encourage our seeming separation from the Source, we must take responsibility for the energetic effects of our choice.

There is danger ahead because the ego-construct, mistakenly fearing that transformation means its annihilation, will fight to maintain its superiority using all the tricks and wiles that the mind has learned over a lifetime. To avoid its artful promptings, we will have to let go of the ego's need to heal and help others, to let go of doing the right thing, let go of anxiety about failure, let go of becoming a healer like Yeshua and Maryam, let go of the need for their approval or the approval of any others, let go of the need to prove ourselves, let go of the voice of disapproval. The path is about relaxing and letting go. Just as we can feel the muscles and tendons of our body relaxing as we let go of stress and tension, so we can translate the feelings of relaxation and letting go to our thoughts and emotions. Breathing is the key here, for the breath can carry energy, allowing us to breathe out negativity, stress, and tension, and inhale the life-giving energies of the Source.

Maryam said: "I am here." During my research I found her words resonating with something very strong and very ancient. Now, I wonder if she was also meaning: "Realize that I AM is here, within each of us." We touched on the Dialogue of the Savior in chapter 3. In the Dialogue, Maryam—having been described by Yeshua as the one who reveals the Revealer—asks him if there is a place devoid of the Revealer. In a reply full of his characteristic humor and wisdom, Yeshua says: "The place where I AM is not!" (140:62:19).

Maryam's Teaching Story draws our attention with Yeshua mentioning *signs*. Even though the Galilean crowd has been given signs pointing to Yeshua's message, they seemed to have missed what was right in front of them. Instead they have focused on his wonder-working without understanding how the miraculous was possible: another clue about how Maryam intended her listeners to work with the teachings. The "miracles" are the signs pointing to the transformational teachings. This is where our focus should be.

TO SUM UP

WHO IS YOUR I AM?

Just as in Sign Four, the counsel is to examine your doubts carefully—any trace of doubt prevents the universe from giving you its full support. Now is the time to recall that with a firm intention centered in the heart, we can create. The people can be fed and the people can be healed. It is the time when we must relax into what may seem like a misty world of trust and faith. It is the point where many turn back because the "goal" seems out of reach, even though the soul—via the voice of the heart—has been assuring us that there is no goal, there is nothing to be achieved, and there is only the realization of who we truly are, only being in that mode of awareness. The mind questions: How can there be no goal? What am I striving for then? What is the point? These questions are like asking those in a dance why they are dancing and what will they achieve by dancing? Can we understand the dancer who turns to us with a loving expression and smiling face saying: "We are dancing for the sheer joy of dancing!"

We live in times when meaning is paramount. How about this for meaning: Yeshua really meant it when he said that the link between your personal I am and the ancient declaration given to Moses is that I AM is present in the physical cosmos—as you, as me, as All That Is—for the sheer fun and joy of it!

LIVING IN SHACKS

There is a long interlude between the lessons of Sign Five, Yeshua's teaching about the I AM, and Sign Six. The interlude starts with Yeshua continuing his stay in the Galilee. At this point in her Story, Maryam reveals some of the reasons for her later leadership of the Jesus movement, and her impending grief begins to surface. There are groups of people in Judea, who at that time were the only people known as "the Jews," who wanted to punish or even kill Yeshua, so he hesitated to go to Jerusalem a third time, even for the festival pilgrimage of Sukkot: "the Jewish festival of Booths." This might have been a difficult decision for him since biblical evidence alone suggests that he was probably born on the first day of Sukkot in 5 BCE, during our month of September.

(John 7:1–14) After this Jesus went about in Galilee. He did not wish to go about in Judea because the Jews were looking for an opportunity to kill him. Now the Jewish festival of Booths was near. So his brothers said to him, "Leave here and go to Judea so that your disciples also may see the works you are doing; for no one who wants to be widely known acts in secret. If you do these things, show yourself to the world." (For not even his brothers believed in him.) Jesus said to them, "My time has not yet come, but your time is always here. The world cannot hate you, but it hates me because I testify against it that its works are evil. Go to the festival yourselves. I am not going to this festival, for my time has not yet fully come." After saying this, he remained in Galilee: But after his brothers had gone to the festival, then he also went, not publicly but as it were in secret. The Jews were looking for him at the festival and saying, "Where is he?" And there was considerable complaining about him among the crowds. While some were saying, "He is a good man," others were saying, "No, he is deceiving the crowd." Yet no one would speak openly about him for fear of the Jews. About the middle of the festival Jesus went up into the temple and began to teach.

Many of his unnamed brothers have always been wary of the wild Rabbi. They taunt him in a bid to get him to join them on the pilgrimage south. He can't expect people to know about his teachings if he hides himself in his home territory, they say. We may wonder just how much his brothers really cared about him, knowing that Judea was no longer a safe place for him and his friends. But a shaman-prophet of Yeshua's stature would be unconcerned about being "widely known."

Visit a respected shaman, healer, or holy person today and you will see that this is still true. They know very well that, if necessary, their energies can have the effect of bringing the world to their door.

Yeshua did not want to miss the pilgrimage to celebrate Sukkot, but thought it prudent to slip into Jerusalem without his skeptical brothers. There seemed to be a number of anomalies in the text, such as Yeshua's need to go "as it were in secret" to avoid the numerous groups who were out searching for him, yet by the middle of the week-long festival, he was to be found openly teaching in the Temple.

From here until the end of chapter 8 in the Gospel of Signs, there is a change of pace as well as the tone of its content, presenting long speeches by Yeshua to those who have gathered to hear him, and his extended responses to their often confused and angry reactions. Later, we will look at the change in the Gospel of Signs, but before that we need to tease out the reason why Maryam particularly mentions Yeshua wanting to celebrate the festival that marks Rosh Hashanah (literally: "the beginning of the year").

HARVESTTIME AND LETTING GO

As New Year celebrations begin, Rosh Hashanah is a reminder that renewal means acceptance and acknowledgement of what has passed. In this five-part autumn festival, with its roots in agricultural thanksgiving, people examine the "fields" of their lives to see where fresh growth needs to be seeded, where whatever no longer nourishes spiritual life is weeded out, where the harvest of personal and earthly gifts can be celebrated by a return to simplicity, where talents can be encouraged and commitments made to water the fields of daily life, and where the past is not forgotten or left behind but rather transformed.

Five days after Yom Kippur—the day of making amends—the joyful five-day festival of Sukkot commemorates the time of wandering in the wilderness, before the Israelites finally settled on a homeland. During that time of wandering, if they didn't have a stout tent, people built makeshift dwellings from whatever they could find. In Hebrew a *sukkah* (pl. *sukkot*) is literally a shack or shed made of whatever vegetation you can get hold of. Traditional Jewish people today still create makeshift structures, or even have a dedicated shed in which to celebrate the festival—a time to eat, drink, and sleep "under the sky" in their homemade sukkah. As you can imagine, it's a great time for children or any adult with a childlike disposition.

WILDERNESS FINDS
MEANING IN THE HEART

Maryam has drawn our attention again to the call of the wild and a celebration of wilderness. Her mention of this time in her Story is significant, for the theme of arduous wandering in the wilderness appears again with the pilgrimage south to celebrate how her ancestors lived in simple huts during their long journey through time and space, from captivity to freedom, across a great desert. Furthermore, pilgrims set off for the sacred place at the heart of their religion—the temple of Jerusalem—to take part in honoring Sukkot.

Sukkot is a time to celebrate overcoming adversity and the end of wandering. We are counseled to travel inward, to the temple of our heart center, to look at what we have overcome so far and to realize we can end our "wandering" now that we have found the path to the heart. Are we still captives to how we were before the pilgrimage or is our wandering leading to a new freedom?

TO SUM UP

YOUR HARVEST AND A FESTIVAL OF JOY

Before we move on toward Sign Six, we need to take note of the seasonal signs to gather in our own "harvest." At this time the theme of harvest is joined with the theme of release, seen in the release of leaves by deciduous trees. Release is the letting go of anything that is blocking the way to personal transformation. While the actual harvest is celebrated, the events of personal life are gathered in. Letting go also means acceptance of death, as the trees accept the fall of their leaves. In the physical world there can be no life without death, but as the trees tell us, life begins again in the following spring.

As Maryam's Teaching Story progresses, our understanding of wilderness as a place of resonation and self-discovery deepens. This is the place where the Israelites first heard a new name for, and a new concept of, the Source; the place where Moses the shaman realized that he was part of I AM. Sukkot is the great celebration of the ancestral time in the wilderness when people can take stock of all the insights they have gained from being "in the wilderness." When we have managed to let go, as counseled in Sign Five and again during this time of harvest, we discover that Sukkot is a festival of joy. Maryam would have reminded her followers that the festival also teaches that pleasure is essential to our well-being.

MORE RUMBLES IN THE TEMPLE

The authenticity of much of the material in the Fourth Gospel's chapter 7 and most of chapter 8 is still in dispute among scholars. To many both chapters seem like later insertions to align with and emphasize the Christian account of events leading up to the Crucifixion. The text that has come down to us today both sounds and feels unlike the rest of the Gospel of Signs. It is difficult to imagine Maryam narrating Yeshua's long conversations in the Jerusalem synagogues as part of her Teaching Story. It seems that whatever her teachings were regarding Yeshua's last days in Judea, they have been swamped by an account of the fiery disputes he was having with both religious officials and pious synagogue-goers.

In both chapters Yeshua makes a number of attempts to explain his revolutionary teachings about the Source and an individual's sacred reality. As usual these fall on deaf ears, and it is apparent that tension is building toward what we know will be a final showdown with the Temple authorities. But among these lengthy exchanges, some real gems may still be identified by the characteristic ring of Maryam's wisdom. For example, in the closing verses of chapter 8, during a row with the crowd, the figure of Abraham—often thought of as the "first Jew"— is mentioned ten times, culminating in Yeshua's startling declaration: "Very truly, I tell you, before Abraham was, I am." This remark is way beyond their understanding and the crowd of Judeans is so baffled and outraged that they pick up stones to throw at him—so presumably they were outside at this point in the account. Yeshua realizes that it's time to make a swift exit (Gospel of Signs 8:57–59).

It was as if Yeshua, exasperated by their closed minds, said to his antagonists: "Don't keep banging on about Abraham. This is a temple, a sacred space we're in right now. I'm talking about the spiritual part of us, the part that existed even *before* Abraham—the I AM. Get it?" Like the deep meaning of Sukkot, this Aramaic koan: "Before Abraham was, I am" follows directly from Yeshua's teaching about I AM and the I AM Presence within all of us. Maryam wants her followers to make contact again with the deep truth that she introduced at the beginning of her Teaching Story: Who or what existed before the "first Jew," as a metaphor for the first human being?

TO SUM UP

YOU EXISTED BEFORE
WHO YOU THINK YOU ARE

For most of the Fourth Gospel, Yeshua has been talking about the spiritual aspect of himself, his own I AM Presence. From the point of view of Maryam's Teaching Story, this is inevitable for he is the symbol of the sacred soul, your sacred soul. Centuries before him, Moses had grasped the same concept—that I AM existed before any human being, even before Creation. But to really "get it" we have to be able to see with the eye of the heart.

15

Sign Six

SPITTING ON CLAY

I Was Blind, but Now I See • You Are Gods

The scene changes as we move to Sign Six and the cornerstone of Maryam's teaching. It is Shabbat. We have left the center of the city of controversy where it has been so dangerous, and we see that Yeshua and the followers are walking the road that runs outside the city walls.

I WAS BLIND, BUT NOW I SEE

(John 9:1–39) As he walked along, he saw a man blind from birth. His disciples asked him, "Rabbi, who sinned, this man or his parents, that he was born blind?" Jesus answered, "Neither this man nor his parents sinned; he was born blind so that God's works might be revealed in him. We must work the works of him who sent me while it is day; night is coming when no one can work. As long as I am in the world, I am the light of the world." When he had said this, he spat on the ground and made mud with the saliva and spread the mud on the man's eyes, saying to him, "Go, wash in the pool of Siloam" (which means Sent). Then he went and washed and came back able to see. The neighbors and those who had seen him before as a beggar began to ask, "Is this not the man who used to sit and beg?" Some were saying, "It is he." Others were saying, "No, but it is someone like him." He kept saying, "I am the man." But they kept asking him, "Then how were your eyes opened?" He answered, "The man called Jesus made mud, spread it on my eyes, and said to me, 'Go to Siloam and wash.' Then I went and washed and received my sight." They said to him, "Where is he?" He said, "I do not know." They brought to the Pharisees the man who had formerly been blind. Now it was a Sabbath day when Jesus made the mud and opened his eyes. Then the Pharisees also began to ask him how he had received his sight. He said to them, "He put mud on my eyes. Then I washed, and now I see." Some of the Pharisees said, "This man is not from God, for he does not observe the Sabbath." But others said, "How can a man who is a sinner perform such signs?" And they were divided. So they said again to the blind man, "What do you say about him? It was your eyes he opened." He said, "He is a prophet." The Jews did not believe that he had been blind and had received his sight until they called the parents of the man who had received his sight and asked them, "Is this your son, who you say was born blind? How then does he now see?" His parents answered, "We know that this is our son, and that he was born blind; but we do not know how it is that now he sees, nor do we know who opened his eyes. Ask him; he is of age. He will speak for himself." His parents said this because they were afraid of the Jews; for the Jews had already agreed that anyone who confessed Jesus to be the Messiah would be put out of the synagogue. Therefore his parents said, "He is of age; ask him." So for the second time they called the man who had been blind, and they said to him, "Give glory to God! We know that this man is a sinner." He answered, "I do not know whether he is a sinner. One thing I do know, that though I was blind, now I see." They said to him, "What did he do to you? How did he open your eyes?" He answered them, "I have told you already, and you would not listen. Why do you want to hear it again? Do you also want to become his disciples?" Then they reviled him, saying, "You are his disciple, but we are disciples of Moses. We know that God has spoken to Moses, but as for this man, we do not know where he comes from." The man answered, "Here is an astonishing thing! You do not know where he comes from, and yet he opened my eyes. We know that God does not listen to sinners, but he does listen to one who worships him and obeys his will. Never since the world began has it been heard that anyone opened the eyes of a person born blind. If this man were not from God, he could do nothing." They answered him, "You were born entirely in sins, and are you trying to teach us?" And they drove him out. Jesus heard that they had driven him out, and when he found him, he said, "Do you believe in the Son of Man?" He answered, "And who is he, sir? Tell me, so that I may believe in him." Jesus said to him, "You have seen him, and the one speaking with you is he." He said, "Lord, I believe." And he worshiped him. Jesus said, "I came into this world for judgment so that those who do not see may see, and those who do see may become blind."

Yeshua cannot escape those in need, knowing that every encounter with another, whether sick or whole, has a purpose. When his followers ask whether the man's blindness is a cause of wrongdoing, Yeshua answers: "He was not born blind because of something he did in a past life neither are his parents the cause of his blindness. You must realize the ways of Alahah (the Source). Some souls come here with infirmities. The sacred soul is untouched by such things. The soul may come here to know how it is to live with infirmity. Further, such great souls offer others the chance to show love and compassion. This may be the soul's purpose. But most of all you must realize that souls choose whether or not to come to Earth."

In shamanic and healing spirituality, you do not *have* a soul, you *are* a soul. Hebrew spirituality has the same perspective. Yeshua's answer confuses some of the group and makes others unhappy. What did he mean when he spoke of soul? Still others pondered on his words.

Yeshua heals the blind man, who tells his friends that he has been made whole. This attracts the ire of some in the crowd, who advise the Parushim (Pharisees; the Jewish officials) that someone has sinned by healing on the Sabbath, a stoning offense. The man who was blind defends Yeshua. In doing so the young man angers the Parushim, who throw him onto the street.

Yeshua hears about the rumpus, and a few of the followers set out to find the young man who had been blind. When Yeshua sees him, he claps him on the shoulder. "Well done. You were not afraid of them. They've got a problem with you. They can't believe what's under their noses. Do you believe it's possible for an ordinary human being to use divine power to heal?" "Of course I'm sure it's possible. I've heard of healers, they're everywhere. But someone who can open the eyes of the blind that's something else. Is that the work of an ordinary human being like me, I don't think so." "You're looking at an ordinary human being just like you." The young man smiles broadly. "So it was you, I thought I recognized your voice. Of course I can believe in you, I'm so grateful. May the Holy One bless you, sir." The young man kneels down and touches Yeshua's feet with his forehead. Yeshua hastily lifts him up. "May your sight help you to believe in the power of the Holy One, which is within every being. Peace be with you, my friend." "And also with you!" the young man replies. As he says this, Yeshua turns to us his followers and smiles. In the story he tells them that the young man has had his inner eyes opened.

The real unfortunates in the story were those who thought that they could see, in the sense of knowing all about the sacred, yet when the evidence of the sacred was in front of them, they failed to see. Would they even recognize the sacred if it jumped up and hit them between the eyes? The words of William Blake in *The Marriage of Heaven and*

Hell sum up the solution to their dilemma: "If the doors of perception were cleansed every thing would appear to man as it is, Infinite. For man has closed himself up . . ."

EVERY DAY IS SACRED

Again, we are being assured that every day is indeed sacred. However, it is worthwhile keeping a special day for contemplation of the sacred. The Hebrew word *shabbat* contains a root meaning "rest," especially after the completion of something. Thus there is a day when we cannot only rest but can contemplate the great completion that is our soul and where our soul comes from. The greeting of peace that we give each other on that day also brings remembrance. The completed person is at peace on every level of their being—they are in balance within themselves and in harmony with their surroundings. Keeping such a special day makes it a day of nourishment on every level.

A STORY ABOUT HAVING "NEW EYES"

Maryam takes time to tell the story of the blind man in detail. This signals to us that the story has many layers. Yeshua teaches about sight and seeing, yes, and as we listen, we realize that everything we have experienced so far has been leading to the meaning of this pivotal event. We are revisiting the theme of being born again, a key theme in Maryam's Teaching Story. Earlier in our healing this meant our realizing that each of us is a divine being. When people practice this realization, they open their inner eyes, they see with the eyes of the soul. As Marcel Proust observed, the real voyage of discovery consists not in seeking new landscapes, but in having new eyes.

The story of the young man born blind describes the life of any person. They live their lives as if their ego-construct, with its personality, is who they really are. They are blind to their spiritual reality. It is common for parents to reinforce this when they, too, are blind to their spiritual reality. Then something happens that gives a person the opportunity to experience this reality.

Slowly the light dawns, while others may scoff as the world seems to deny any other view. There is the Oneness, there are holy people, and there are ordinary human beings. Yeshua teaches that when one sees with the eyes of the soul, with the eye of the heart, it becomes apparent that all these are the same—a very hard lesson to grasp. The religious authorities know that they will lose their power if the people understand such spiritual truth. They hold on to their power by branding those who speak this truth as evil. However, those who receive even the smallest hint of who they are will not be fooled, for now the voice of the soul may be heard within.

UNDERSTANDING SUFFERING
AND THE "NEGATIVES" OF LIFE

Finally, the Rabbi gives a teaching that goes to the heart of life. Life is a mystery because we do not understand the soul, and we do not understand that the source of all things in the cosmos is Sacred Unity. We look at life from our perspective in which any suffering is bad and happiness is good. From this perspective, how can the Source allow suffering? If I AM allows suffering, what does this tell us? Yet people are quite happy for the Source to allow them to enjoy life. What does that mean? If we cannot understand the meaning of suffering and happiness, how then can we understand why some souls are born with infirmities, into poverty or misfortune while others are born with good health, into riches or good fortune?

In Sign One we were shown that the world is a world of opposites. It cannot be otherwise. This is how it is. This is why the soul comes here—to experience life where there can be the opposite of Oneness, in every possible form of the opposite, even the opposite of love. Thus darkness appears to have its opposite: light. Heat has its opposite: cold. People feel that the opposite of the good is the bad. So if there is happiness and joy, there is going to be sadness and suffering, until we remember the lesson of the first dream story—the reality is that all is Oneness. And once we see with the eyes of the soul, Oneness becomes our experience and we can accept the appearance of duality as simply how it is in our world. Yeshua called that "entering the kingdom." When your inner eyes are opened, you indeed enter the beautiful and magical realm of Sacred Unity where it becomes clear that God *is* every being—the ant, the flower, the human—not some superhuman manipulator, watching like a perverted voyeur as it endorses and allows the suffering within its creation.

Yeshua was often in that kingdom and, to help people understand the truth of suffering, talked about it as if it was part of his everyday experience. But people misunderstood him and said he was claiming to be a king.

FORGETTING AND RECONNECTION

The person born blind from birth symbolizes the fact that we are born into a form of life where we quickly forget our spiritual reality as the demands of the physical grow ever stronger. In a state common to most of us, we don't see things as they are; we see them as *we* are. To be "healed" of that condition and situation is to reenter the realm of the miraculous, the place where one sees with the eyes of the soul.

There is an old Jewish story that I wish they had told me during my early days at school. Before you hear it, go and look at yourself in the mirror and find the philtrum, the little depression that runs from the base of your nose to the top of your lip. Put a finger there to remind you where it is. The story says that before we are born, we know everything. We know our connection to the Source, and we know our unity with All That Is. We know the whole cosmos. We even know the past and the future. Then, when we are born, an angel touches our top lip and we forget everything. In this way we start life afresh, without the influence of what we already know. The angel's touch leaves that depression below the nose. We get on with our life. Then one day there comes a time when we can hear what is going on inside us. We get that "something is missing" feeling. The more we feel it, the more intense the memory of something missing becomes.

What the angel mark does, says the story, is help us remember what is missing: our deep connection to the soul-self, to one another, to life, and to the Source. This remembrance is the call of the soul. It tells us that we came to manifest the sacred, not the personality alone. Our personality is what the soul chooses to manifest *through*. The little dent above the top lip is a visual reminder about reconnection, even a way back "home." If you can see this, you can see with new eyes. I think that if little worried Jack had heard this story, it would have taken him back to the beach vision and the safety of his Heart Space.

You may be wondering if you ever went into your Heart Space. Think back. Sometimes you may have experienced some form of the loveless, have been a receiver of abuse, injustice, neglect. You may have been hurt, and your reaction may have been to stop feeling to survive. But your feelings of confusion, disappointment, and disillusion tell you that you went into your Heart Space. What you unconsciously did was compare the behavior of others with your inner sense of love, justice, and oneness. They did not match up, hence the confusion and sadness. In time we may think we know how other people operate, how the world operates. We do not need to compare how things should be anymore. When life gets too painful, we may forget, block the way through, or avoid the beautiful retreat we have inside and instead seek solace elsewhere. Of course, this takes us away from the Heart Space and so our connection with the sacred. Looking back you may be able to pinpoint actual events that tell you when you began to lose your connection.

THE SOUL'S WORK IS TO DIRECT OUR PATH

In Maryam's Teaching Story, the followers question Yeshua about the causes of blindness. In doing so the text reveals that people of the time understood concepts like life after death and past lives as well as the possibility of inherited characteristics. Is the young man's blindness due to something inherited from his parents, or caused by his parents, his own past deeds, or even his own past life? All these are possible, says Yeshua. But he does not want them to miss the deeper issue: we do not really see that all life is God, and that it is the sacred soul directing the path of each individual. In terms of our own journey, the fact that others may not appreciate this is irrelevant. The real, if difficult, challenge then is to align with soul rather than agonize over causes of conditions.

The inner meaning of the Sign Six episode is that human beings tend to be blind to their spiritual reality until their *clouded inner vision* is cleared or restored by heeding the call of the soul. Sign Six is a turning point on the healing journey. We hear echoes of the creative beginning as all the elements of Maryam's Teaching Story come together in a typically shamanic form of healing with the use of a healing paste. The shaman-healer breathes the sacred life force into the mixture of earth and saliva, the element water.

TO SUM UP

SEEING WITH NEW EYES

Once again we have to see what the "miracle" of the restoration of sight is pointing to. The core of Maryam's teaching is to awaken us to the spiritual reality that calls to us from within. This call can be summed up in the word *see*—to see with the eyes of the soul. In another gospel Yeshua describes our eyes as like a lamp, reflecting the degree of our inner light at any given moment. Healthy or generous eyes, he says, illuminate our entire body (Luke 11:34). This seeing with the eyes of the soul is about a simple or childlike way of seeing the good in people and situations, a way of seeing that is essential to all healing, for seeing the good is seeing the sacred.

Your ability to see in this way is crucial to break out of the bonds of thinking that your personality self is all that you are. Every experience of the Divine begins with leaving your ordinary way of perceiving the world, leaving the way with which you may be comfortable, to enter a more vulnerable and open state. When you break with the ordinary and the comfortable, transformation begins and healing happens.

YOU ARE GODS

Yeshua's teachings explain that we are all gods, because we are the Oneness of the Creator and Creation. Maryam's listeners can look behind the words and understand, but the Pharisees and others cannot comprehend. One key to knowing the Way is understanding the concept of sin and what it means for Yeshua in the story of the blind man.

WHAT IS "SIN"?

The young man, healed of blindness, is again surrounded by the Pharisees who, predictably, take his healing as a personal slight.

(John 9:40–41) Some of the Pharisees near him heard this and said to him, "Surely we are not blind, are we?" Jesus said to them, "If you were blind, you would not have sin. But now that you say, 'We see,' your sin remains."

Here, Yeshua's use of the word "sin" needs to be understood in its Aramaic context, where the word originates in archery. The word is not used by Yeshua as a judgment, for sin is about missing the mark, not getting it, for whatever reasons. As we have already seen, the riddle he sets them is a typical Semitic teaching style and way of speaking. Listeners are left to solve the riddle themselves rather than have the answer given them. Indeed, Maryam herself uses the same technique in her own teaching. In Sign One, for example, the riddle may seem obvious: How is it possible to turn water for ritual washing into the best wine? But, at a deeper level, the riddle becomes: Why turn water for ritual washing into the best wine? Or: What was really going on when water for ritual washing was turned into the best wine?

We are told over and over again that Yeshua does not judge so that the existing text has either been altered to fit dogmatic assertions or the scribes and translators just did not understand what he was saying and the way that he was saying it. When working with any revered text like the Fourth Gospel, it is always worth asking who was around to witness what is in the text and, just as importantly, who was able to commit it to writing? Then: Who decided to change it? The Pharisees don't get it and so Yeshua tries to help them with a different approach to the riddle.

(John 10:1–21) "Very truly, I tell you, anyone who does not enter the sheepfold by the gate but climbs in by another way is a thief and a bandit. The one who enters by the gate is the shepherd of the sheep. The gatekeeper opens the gate for him, and the sheep hear his voice. He calls his own sheep by name and leads them out. When he has brought out all his own, he goes ahead of them, and the sheep follow him because they know his voice. They will not follow a stranger, but they will run from him because they do not know the voice of strangers." Jesus used this figure of speech with them, but they did not understand what he was saying to them. So again Jesus said to them, "Very truly, I tell you, I am the gate for the sheep. All who came before me are thieves and bandits; but the sheep did not listen to them. I am the gate. Whoever enters by me will be saved, and will come in and go out and find pasture. The thief comes only to steal and kill and destroy. I came that they may have life and have it abundantly. I am the good shepherd. The good shepherd lays down his life for the sheep. The hired hand, who is not the shepherd and does not own the sheep, sees the wolf coming and leaves the sheep and runs away—and the wolf snatches them and scatters them. The hired hand runs away because a hired hand does not care for the sheep. I am the good shepherd. I know my own, and my own know me, just as the Father knows me and I know the Father. And I lay down my life for the sheep. I have other sheep that do not belong to this fold. I must bring them also, and they will listen to my voice. So there will be one flock, one shepherd. For this reason the Father loves me, because I lay down my life in order to take it up again. No one takes it from me, but I lay it down of my own accord. I have power to lay it down, and I have power to take it up again. I have received this command from my Father." Again the Jews were divided because of these words. Many of them were saying, "He has a demon and is out of his mind. Why listen to him?" Others were saying, "These are not the words of one who has a demon. Can a demon open the eyes of the blind?"

Since the healing of the man born blind, Yeshua continues to provoke both the religious authorities and people in the crowds that gather to listen to his teachings. We need to bear in mind that argument and debate were very much part of the oral teaching scene at the time, just as it still is today. People are entitled to their opinion as much as the teacher; further, the purpose of argument and debate is to challenge teachers to explore and expand their teachings and clarify difficult points. Hence many of the passages in the Gospel of Signs have this element. In the one above (John 10:1–21), for example, Yeshua's conversation with the Pharisees now takes an important new turn, where Yeshua compares both himself and the I AM to a conscientious and caring shepherd.

I AM SHOWS THE WAY

In the Middle East the shepherd goes ahead of the sheep and leads them so that this familiar image would resonate with people of the time.

Having attracted and gathered in his audience, Yeshua moves the imagery forward. I AM is not only the Way, he says, but also the gateway that leads to the Way—to the experience of Oneness, or the "Kingdom of Heaven." The Pharisees and their friends are losing ground. Their feeble retort is that Yeshua's images of I AM are the ravings of a madman. But others in the crowd are not that gullible. Madmen cannot cure blindness.

Maryam's Teaching Story has put a truth right in front of her followers. The crowd's statement about blindness is carefully placed so that it comes at the end of the teaching about the I AM. The last thing we hear is a sign pointing to a deeper teaching about the meaning of inner blindness—the failure to see that we are each a part of the Divine, imbued with divine consciousness.

DAIMONS AND DEMONS

And now to the controversial word "demon" whose original meaning has been subverted. In Greek, a *daimon* is "a divine entity" or "an inspiration." Having a daimon gave a person the ability to receive and interpret spirit, or the good fortune to have divine forces directing the path of life. Christian texts translate the word as an illness, disease, evil spirit, or something very negative. Thus the word became a Christian denial of the God within. When we are totally ignorant of our sacred reality, all seven levels of consciousness, as represented by the energy centers, are asleep, shut down, even inactive, as if a negative force— now called a *demon*—resides in each. Hence Maryam is described by the writer of the Luke gospel as a woman from whom seven demons have been driven. When we apply the original meaning of demon as the indwelling spirit or life force of the seven energy centers, an exciting portrait of Maryam is revealed. She is the woman in whom the seven levels of consciousness are activated and then released into the world, for she has the ability to receive and interpret information and knowledge from the world of spirit. You will recall that we know this about her through the Nag Hammadi scriptures.

THE TRUTH ABOUT ONENESS

(John 10:22–30) At that time the festival of the Dedication took place in Jerusalem. It was winter, and Jesus was walking in the temple, in the portico of Solomon. So the Jews gathered around him and said to him, "How long will you keep us in suspense? If you are the Messiah, tell us plainly." Jesus answered, "I have told you, and you do not believe. The works that I do in my Father's name testify to me; but you do not believe, because you do not belong to my sheep. My sheep hear my voice. I know them, and they follow me. I give them eternal life, and they will never perish. No one will snatch them out of my hand. What my Father has given me is greater than all else, and no one can snatch it out of the Father's hand. The Father and I are one."

The time of the healing of the blind man was autumn, but verses 22 and 23 make an interesting point of chronology by stating "at that time the festival of the Dedication took place in Jerusalem. It was winter, and Jesus was walking in the temple, in the portico of Solomon." The festival of the Dedication, now known as Hannukah, commemorated the reconsecration of the Temple, in a light festival originally linked to the winter solstice. It seems as if these lines were part of the original text because of the mention of Solomon. Will Maryam's listeners be reminded of the lost wisdom of the great Solomon?

Whatever the reason for the jump in time, we have to go with the text as it stands today. But again, we may pause to ponder over the question of inserts and redaction. We can recall that Yeshua originally went to Jerusalem for the *autumnal* festival of Sukkot. He is a wanted man in Jerusalem yet, the writer tells us, Yeshua is still around for the celebration of Hannukah in *winter,* and is apparently continuing a "conversation" that has lasted around three months! Thus, following quickly on from the seasonal insert, the text continues with Yeshua's theme of

I AM as a good shepherd, ending his controversial remarks with the existential bombshell: "The Father and I are one." Has he really blown it this time?

(John 10:31–39) The Jews took up stones again to stone him. Jesus replied, "I have shown you many good works from the Father. For which of these are you going to stone me?" The Jews answered, "It is not for a good work that we are going to stone you, but for blasphemy, because you, though only a human being, are making yourself God." Jesus answered, "Is it not written in your law, 'I said, you are gods?' If those to whom the word of God came were called 'gods'—and the scripture cannot be annulled—can you say that the one whom the Father has sanctified and sent into the world is blaspheming because I said, 'I am God's Son'?" Then they tried to arrest him again, but he escaped from their hands.

But the crowd, no doubt egged on by religious officials in the background, cannot cope with his responses and gather stones to throw at him. Before they can do this, Yeshua shouts a quotation from Asaf the psalmist: "I said, you are gods!" Since this is a quotation from Psalm 82, it is hardly likely that Yeshua would have said *your law,* two words that stand out as a later insert. However, both phrases would have incensed a crowd brought up with the idea of separation from the Source, and Yeshua is forced to use the ensuing confusion to flee for his life. Who had the courage to witness the episode? It is difficult to imagine an out-of-breath Yeshua rejoining his followers panting: "Guess what I've been saying to that mob back there? I nearly got stoned!"

Maryam's sense of drama is quite deliberate. She alerts her listeners to Yeshua's simple statement about Oneness/Sacred Unity that has been misunderstood throughout the centuries by those who need the illusion of separation. His teaching about I AM is part of his revolutionary message. Then Maryam reinforces her point with a reference to the beloved

Psalms. Asaf lived a thousand years before Yeshua and was the musical director who set most of David's poetic prayers to music. He used music to enter into a trance state, but he is noted for the bitterness of his lamentations, and in Psalm 82, he is expressing his disillusionment with the Solomon who became obsessed with material wealth and power and shelved his heart-centered wisdom.

In the lament the I AM reminds the people that they are divine beings and are therefore responsible for themselves and their own lives. Using the memory and meaning of Asaf's words, and Yeshua's teaching about Oneness, Maryam takes us back to Sign One and the deep meaning of marriage. In this way she prompts her listeners to recall their spiritual reality—we are gods *because* each of us and I AM are one. Secondly, this is why healing is possible, whether hands-on or at a distance. The whole episode calls to mind the words of the Indian avatar Sai Baba (1926–2011) who frequently assured people: "I am God and you are God. The only difference between us is that I know and experience this while you do not." Again, words that continue to baffle or be misunderstood by those who do not "get it"!

At this turning point in the pilgrimage, in a world that may seem to have turned its back on spiritual values, we need to be very aware of our responsibility to ourselves and the community. Thus, the outcome of working with the final, Seventh Sign depends on our ability to see with the eyes of the soul.

HEADING BACK TO THE BEGINNING

(John 10:40–42) He went away again across the Jordan to the place where John had been baptizing earlier, and he remained there. Many came to him, and they were saying, "John performed no sign, but everything that John said about this man was true." And many believed in him there.

Yeshua and his followers make their way toward "the place where John had been baptizing"—the area near Bethany. Like the symbol of the ouroboros, this is the place of death and rebirth, where alpha meets omega; or the Hebrew *alef* meets *tav*, the last letter, known as the Seal of Creation. We are revisiting the imaginal place where we prepared for our transformational pilgrimage, though things are not quite the same. John the Immerser is no longer there, but people still gather on the banks of the Jordan where he used to teach. Some are overheard confirming that what he said about Yeshua was true.

TO SUM UP

THE CHOICE TO REALIZE AND EXPERIENCE I AM WITHIN

Maryam is preparing us for the last big push. At this later stage in our pilgrimage, the symbol of John has disappeared—the time for clearing ourselves of old and stale energies has passed. The Signs Story is not about John, though he was the necessary figure who alerted us to the need for preparation and the need for spending time in the Wilderness. During our travels to and from Judea and the Galilee, accounts of the simple but revolutionary message of Yeshua and Maryam have gotten back to this remote place. The good news is that the Way ahead is clear and can be relied on. We have come this far. Recall that you have an inner messiah because you are a sacred being. Your soul is your inner messiah. It is time, then, to slip the bonds that bound you like grave clothes and break out of the cave—or is it? The choice is still yours.

16

Sign Seven

BREAKING OUT AND RESURRECTION

Maryam's Teaching Story opens up to begin its final, startling climax. We are in Judea, outside Jerusalem, on the east bank of the Jordan where John had once been immersing people. We stop and make camp. Many come and welcome us saying they have heard about Yeshua's teaching and healing, especially the man born blind. A messenger arrives from the nearby village of Bethany, where Maryam's Teaching Story began.

(John 11:1–46) Now a certain man was ill, Lazarus of Bethany, the village of Mary and her sister Martha. Mary was the one who anointed the Lord with perfume and wiped his feet with her hair; her brother Lazarus was ill. So the sisters sent a message to Jesus, "Lord, he whom you love is ill." But when Jesus heard it, he said, "This illness does not lead to death; rather it is for God's glory, so that the Son of God may be glorified through it." Accordingly, though Jesus loved Martha and her sister and Lazarus, after having heard that Lazarus was ill, he stayed two days longer in the place where he was. Then after this he said to the disciples, "Let

190

us go to Judea again." The disciples said to him, "Rabbi, the Jews were just now trying to stone you, and are you going there again?" Jesus answered, "Are there not twelve hours of daylight? Those who walk during the day do not stumble, because they see the light of this world. But those who walk at night stumble, because the light is not in them." After saying this, he told them, "Our friend Lazarus has fallen asleep, but I am going there to awaken him." The disciples said to him, "Lord, if he has fallen asleep, he will be all right." Jesus, however, had been speaking about his death, but they thought that he was referring merely to sleep. Then Jesus told them plainly, "Lazarus is dead. For your sake I am glad I was not there, so that you may believe. But let us go to him." Thomas, who was called the Twin, said to his fellow disciples, "Let us also go, that we may die with him." When Jesus arrived, he found that Lazarus had already been in the tomb four days. Now Bethany was near Jerusalem, some two miles away, and many of the Jews had come to Martha and Mary to console them about their brother. When Martha heard that Jesus was coming, she went and met him, while Mary stayed at home. Martha said to Jesus, "Lord, if you had been here, my brother would not have died. But even now I know that God will give you whatever you ask of him." Jesus said to her, "Your brother will rise again." Martha said to him, "I know that he will rise again in the resurrection on the last day." Jesus said to her, "I am the resurrection and the life. Those who believe in me, even though they die, will live, and everyone who lives and believes in me will never die. Do you believe this?" She said to him, "Yes, Lord, I believe that you are the Messiah, the Son of God, the one coming into the world." When she had said this, she went back and called her sister Mary, and told her privately, "The Teacher is here and is calling for you." And when she heard it, she got up quickly and went to him. Now Jesus had not yet come to the village, but was still at the place where Martha had met him. The Jews who were with her in the house, consoling her,

saw Mary get up quickly and go out. They followed her because
they thought that she was going to the tomb to weep there. When
Mary came where Jesus was and saw him, she knelt at his feet
and said to him, "Lord, if you had been here, my brother would
not have died." When Jesus saw her weeping, and the Jews who
came with her also weeping, he was greatly disturbed in spirit and
deeply moved. He said, "Where have you laid him?" They said to
him, "Lord, come and see." Jesus began to weep. So the Jews said,
"See how he loved him!" But some of them said, "Could not he
who opened the eyes of the blind man have kept this man from
dying?" Then Jesus, again greatly disturbed, came to the tomb. It
was a cave, and a stone was lying against it. Jesus said, "Take away
the stone." Martha, the sister of the dead man, said to him, "Lord,
already there is a stench because he has been dead four days."
Jesus said to her, "Did I not tell you that if you believed, you would
see the glory of God?" So they took away the stone. And Jesus
looked upward and said, "Father, I thank you for having heard me.
I knew that you always hear me, but I have said this for the sake
of the crowd standing here, so that they may believe that you sent
me." When he had said this, he cried with a loud voice, "Lazarus,
come out!" The dead man came out, his hands and feet bound
with strips of cloth, and his face wrapped in a cloth. Jesus said to
them, "Unbind him, and let him go." Many of the Jews therefore,
who had come with Mary and had seen what Jesus did, believed in
him. But some of them went to the Pharisees and told them what
he had done.

The Story tells how Martha and Maryam, the sisters of Eleazar
(Latin: Lazarus), are begging Yeshua to come to their house where their
brother is seriously ill. We know that Martha and Lazarus are brother
and sister, but, in the last Sign of her Teaching Story, Maryam the storyteller appears as another sister, named Maryam (Mary). Yeshua is not
at all moved by the news. "He'll be all right. His illness won't kill him."

And we stay near the river for another two days. After breakfast Yeshua says: "Why don't we go back to Jerusalem?" The group is dismayed. "What about Lazarus? If we go back to the city you'll be stoned. You'd be crazy to show your face there so soon." "All right," Yeshua says. "Our friend Lazarus has fallen asleep. Instead of going to Jerusalem, I'll go to his place and wake him up."

Thomas apparently mistakes Yeshua's meaning and says it's a long walk, let's leave him to sleep. Yeshua says: "I mean that our friend is thought to be dead." Thomas still doesn't get it and says jauntily: "So let's all go so we can die with him then." This is greeted with laughter.

A quick aside about Thomas, the mystery man who now appears in the Story. His name in Aramaic, Thoma, means "the twin," but the gospels fail to tell us who his other twin was. We lose his original Hebrew name when the Greek translation adds the masculine ending "s" and the twin becomes "Thomas." This name is given to a noncanonical gospel that many find closest to the words of Yeshua in its beauty and profundity (the Gospel of Thomas). Whoever he really was, he had to be very close to the wandering shaman-prophet.

In the story Yeshua knows that Lazarus has been in the family tomb for over three days. The family was well known and many had gathered to mourn and console the sisters. The group has not reached the village when we see Martha running toward them with tears streaming down her face. She is angry with grief and shouts at Yeshua: "Where have you been? If you had come when we sent the message he would still be alive. I thought you loved him. If you are a holy man, you can bring our brother back to us. Say you'll do that."

Yeshua stays calm. "You know there is no death. Your brother will rise again in spirit. You believe that don't you?" "I know all that!" Martha screams. "I want him back again, in his body." In a fury she runs back to the house, pushes through the crowd of mourners and tells her sister, who has been sitting *shivah* ("in mourning"): "The Rabbi is here, Maryam. He's calling for you. If anyone can make him help us it's you. See what you can do." We, and the followers, know who the

Maryam in the Story is, for right at the beginning of the episode, we are told: "Mary was the one who anointed the Lord with perfume and wiped his feet with her hair."

Maryam gets up and goes quickly up the road, followed by some of the mourners. She throws herself at Yeshua's feet and cries: "Lord, if you had come earlier my brother would not have died." Yeshua knows it is Maryam who lies at his feet. His smile changes to concern. Now we are surrounded by weeping and wailing. Yeshua is visibly upset and in tears himself. Someone mutters: "If he could open the eyes of a blind man, surely he could have prevented this death." News travels fast, then, but why did he waste time by the river?

Yeshua says: "Show me where you laid out the body." Everyone makes their way to the family burial cave. As is the custom, a boulder lies in front of the entrance to keep out any animals. "Open it," says Yeshua. Some men roll away the stone. Martha covers her nose and mouth with the edge of her headscarf. She turns to Yeshua. "I'm sorry about the stench. He's been dead four days now." Yeshua says: "You both thought that if I had got here earlier he would have lived. You believe I could have prevented his death?" Martha says: "You are a holy man. You could have asked Alahah to save him." Yeshua whispers: "So you do believe that is possible?" He nods. "Very well."

In the cave the burial cloths bind Lazarus like the paralysis of the man at the healing pool. But, where once he may have been unaware of his soul, or dead to it, he is being awakened by an invisible force coming via Yeshua outside. He is being awakened to his own divine reality. The crowd becomes quiet. Yeshua raises his arms in prayer and then says out loud: "Father I thank you for hearing my prayer." He knows the little crowd needs to hear his prayer because of what is going to happen next. The crowd joins in his "Amen," and then they are astonished when Yeshua shouts into the cave: "Lazarus, come out!"

Lazarus struggles to get up and staggers toward the cave entrance. He is trying to walk with tightly bound legs! There is a shuffling sound, and the crowd gasps as a ghostly figure appears at the entrance—it is

Lazarus bound in his white burial cloths. "Unbind him and let him walk free," says Yeshua. Lazarus is unbound and he walks free.

Even those followers who knew about Yeshua's powers would have been astounded at the outcome of this story. They would have heard stories of wonder-workers who had raised people from the dead, but probably never actually witnessed it, nor known anyone who had witnessed it. The last thing we see is people scurrying off to Jerusalem to inform the Temple authorities about what they think they have witnessed.

TWO, PERHAPS THREE, ASPECTS OF MARYAM

The final episode shows at least two aspects of Maryam. In Aramaic "Martha" means "lady" or "mistress," not in the sense of having servants, but a woman who has some sort of mastery. As "my lady" she is furious with the Rabbi's apparent unconcern about death. She rushes out to confront him with what she feels is his indifference. How could he, her twin soul, be so uncaring as to allow himself to be captured and killed?

Then we see her in the family house at first, as Maryam, like a wife waiting to be summoned. If anyone can get some sense out of the situation, surely it is the woman with whom he constantly demonstrated his love and affection. Again, she finds a way to show us the enduring love between her and Yeshua. Thirdly, as spiritual teacher, she has been the witness to the events she describes and has woven them into a dramatic and memorable story as a gift to her followers and to the world.

In the Story, Yeshua responds not to Martha's anger and recrimination but to the love and grief of Maryam. The third aspect of Maryam is the one that was always free of bonds. Like Martha, the name Maryam contains the Aramaic *maryah,* meaning "someone who has mastery." So in this miracle story, the liberated "brother" is greeted by Maryam in her two aspects of mastery over life as she embodies the energy streams of both feminine and masculine. The three aspects of Maryam are not "dead" because they are conscious of their sacred reality: they experience the realm of the miraculous. Lazarus symbolizes the person who was dead to that reality but is liberated from the thrall of the physical, symbolized by the casting off of the burial clothes. Yeshua is instrumental in this process, representing the special human messenger who has come to help people discover who they really are, to heal their wounds of disconnection from the sacred, and to help them to be reborn into real life and a life of enhanced awareness.

IT'S YOUR DREAM STORY

Your journey has taken you to the opening scene that you experienced some time ago—a place near the river that runs through Judea. In the far distance you can see the hill on which stands the center of the universe: the Temple of Jerusalem. You are near the village called Bet Anyah ("House of the Poor") on the east bank of the river. This village is well known as a place where people with skin diseases, the poor, the disabled, and unwell are cared for, as well as destitute pilgrims on their way to Jerusalem. Even lepers may be found there.

The Teaching Story has come full circle. Now the pilgrim understands what healing is and understands that the worst kind of poverty is the poverty of not knowing that all people are divine. At the beginning of the journey, the "poor" were those attached to the illusion that the physical is all there is. At the end of the journey, you are "poor" because you have jettisoned that baggage and so you appear to have less stuff. But you are also "rich" because you have discovered the true richness of the cosmos, that everything is sacred. You have returned to this place, being able to see it with new eyes. Now that you have completed the circle, you have the opportunity to release yourself and make yourself whole.

Lazarus is alive, so why does the story talk about his death? The dream story was composed for you; it is your dream. In the dream story, the Rabbi has to wait for Lazarus to die to show that a person may be resurrected from the dead state of spiritual ignorance. The miracle of raising a person from the dead has no point if it is merely to show what a wonder-worker he is. There are plenty in this land. The miracle certainly shows the people that the Holy One is present, and powerfully present in the human man Yeshua. But he only works miracles for two main reasons: to demonstrate the love and compassion of the I AM and to draw attention to the fact that I AM is always present in every being. Every being has the khristos, the "anointed one," within them, because every being is the Oneness.

No one but your soul sees that you were bound as well as Lazarus. But your bonds are nothing to do with ignorance of the soul. It feels as if your soul gently and carefully unbinds you. You feel yourself breathing, hear your heart beating. You can move your legs and arms once more. The bonds were your terrible grief about your disconnection from the sacred . . . about everything. You are released!

THE CALL TO RESURRECTION

Your healing is confirmed by your place in the last story in which you return to the village where your pilgrimage to wholeness and harmony began. Here, you return to the theme of being "born again." Maryam shows us two kinds of resurrection through the image of Yeshua. In the first sense he makes it clear that when the physical body dies, the soul cannot die, for it is part of the Source. In the second sense a person may be "dead"—unaware of her divine origin—but it is possible for her to be "resurrected" by discovering her sacred reality, the soul within. Maryam chooses to make these truths an experience that you will remember by setting the story of a death among people she knew and loved.

DEATH AND RESURRECTION

Wherever you are on the planet, there are six directions around you—above, below, before, behind, to the right of you, and to the left of you. The future, including death, lies in the "before" direction. It is one of life's certainties, but a subject generally avoided. Spend some time observing Nature and you will soon realize that death is not only intimately bound up with life, but is essential to living processes.

Our body is a beautiful illustration of the workings of Oneness. Every part of us—from the smallest molecule—works for the good of the whole, the soul's vehicle. Through the network of consciousness, every part of our body is in touch with every other part. We do not have to think about it. But for the life of the body to continue, certain cells are programmed to die. A simple example of our daily unawareness of the necessity of death lies at the surface of our body. A good percentage of dust in any home consists of the dead skin we have sloughed off! Parts of our body are dying every moment as part of the organic process of renewal. Thus we do not have the same body that we had at age ten, and we have largely forgotten the way we used to think at that age.

The death of the body has been with us, then, from the moment of our birth, as a physical and energetic necessity. The secret is that we embrace death, either unconsciously or consciously, in order to continue creating who we are. Physical life and physical death, as aspects of being, are totally compatible. We were spiritual beings before we were conceived, we are spiritual beings while on Earth, and we will be spiritual beings when we leave the body; thus the notion that being stops at the death of the body is an illusion. Resurrection is a fact, not a pious hope. At death your sacred soul has no further need of its physical body; it has moved on.

THE CAVE AS WOMB

My first conscious encounter with Mary Magdalene happened in a cave in the South of France where, according to legend, she lived and continued to teach. The last Sign in her Teaching Story also features a cave: the burial cave of Lazarus. Both of these caves have been wombs, places of gestation. The cave of Sainte Baume acted as the birthplace of my new relationship with Maryam, which, in turn, has birthed this book. In her Teaching Story, the burial cave of Lazarus was the symbol of both being born again and the resurrection of the soul out of the physical body. For me the caves form a continuum that very much reminds me of Maryam's carefully constructed cycle of episodes in the life of her spiritual partner, Yeshua. This prompted me to look at the cave as both womb and catalyst in the development of our spirituality.

CAVES OF REVELATION

In the Palestine of two millennia ago, caves often served as housing for farm animals, and it was undoubtedly in such a cave—or "stable"—that Yeshua was born. Some eight centuries before that event, the setting of the ancient Hebrew book of Melakhim ("Kings") tells a story about the celebrated shaman-prophet Elijah. He had become a thorn in the sides of King Ahab and his wife, Jezebel, who were heavily into idol-worship. They decided to get rid of the holy man and sent him a message to that effect. Fleeing for his life, Elijah took refuge in a cave in the mountainous wilderness of Horev (another name for the place where Moses was given a name for the Source as "I AM"). To make contact with the Holy One, Elijah began to meditate by staring out toward the mouth of the cave. Having had experiences of the divine, he wonders how the Source will present itself. The story tells how he was first confronted by a whirlwind, then an earthquake, and then a raging fire, all of which put him in mortal danger. However, he was not aware of God in any of these natural manifestations. But when the dust had settled and the fire had burnt out, he heard the *kol d'mamah dakah* ("the sound of sheer silence") within himself and knew that he had at last experienced the true nature of the divine (1 Kings 19). This is the subtle voice, or sound, that can only be heard in the silence. Thus the neon-lit sign over the way into our inner cave temple reads: "Be still and know the I AM Presence" (Psalm 46:11).

Caves are given to us by Nature. They were our earliest homes, where we sought safety from animals and other dangers in the outside world. They were where we buried our dead and so they were seen as doorways to the afterlife. It is possible that cave paintings were images of divine revelation or perhaps shamanic communications with divine forces.

Indigenous cultures all revere caves as places where the sacred can be experienced more intensely. Here, the worlds of heaven and Earth meet; all that is above and below, all that is inside and outside become one indivisible reality. I can vouch for all of that, and I discovered for myself that caves can be places of revelation.

TO SUM UP

RESURRECTION NOW

The call of Sign Seven, like the voice of Wisdom in the book of Proverbs, is to resurrect and leave your tomb of ignorance. Throw off the bindings of depending on physical things alone. Become alive and enjoy life as a spiritual being. Express your innate divinity, discover who you really are. Now, being able to see the reality, you are like one being raised from the dead. You can walk out of the tomb in which you had unknowingly placed yourself. Like Lazarus, you may be resurrected, or "born again," but now you have to live as this born-again person. Being born again is about renewal, not denying or burying the past, but renewing the present and so the future.

Your mind, with its conditioning, may not be open to receive and welcome this good news. Be aware that your mind may run through its fears of change and may try to justify them. This is Maryam's warning in the image of people sneaking back to the source of religious power to share their fear with the Temple authorities. But you no longer need to be afraid. The poison of your fear and anger has been washed away. You are free.

17

YOUR
TRANSFORMATION
AND THE NEXT STEP

BACK TO
THE WILDERNESS OF THE HEART

Many reach the end of a pilgrimage only to find that their expectations remain unrealized and their hopes unfulfilled. They feel flat and frustrated. This is a common situation for any pilgrim traveler and is the inevitable outcome of expectation and prejudgment. You thought that you would feel different, perhaps emerge as a "better" person. If you find that you are beating yourself up about this, you have forgotten that the purpose of the Sacred Walk is to do it. But by choosing to return to the Wilderness, you can restore inner balance and peace and recognize your creative place in the Story cycle. Remember the meaning of wilderness: the place that resonates. From there you can look back over the Seven Signs. One or more of them will give you a clue about your feelings. Your feelings are fine. They are not there to be ignored because they are *your* signs, pointing to something that you are trying to tell yourself. But things have changed. You are different. You know where your heart center is, in a deep way. You know it is the place that resonates. You know that you can go there anytime.

MAKE A NEW RELATIONSHIP
WITH THE STORYTELLER

Yeshua and Maryam came together, as man and woman, with a message for all human beings. The story tells us that Maryam and Yeshua are still with us, in spirit. They have many ways of being with you and talking with you. You know this. They have not left you. This awareness can help create a new relationship with them, and you have everything you need to carry that relationship forward. Simply watch out for those who would obstruct you and do what water does: flow around them rather than oppose them. Flow, and keep the waters within you alive.

LIFE IS ABOUT TRANSFORMATION

Life has always been taking you toward transformation—especially spiritual transformation—and this process will go on whatever kind of life you may lead. You may feel that you have been the same person all your life, or you may be aware of the many changes that have formed who you seem to be today. In my early childhood, because my family was always on the move, I felt as if I had lived a number of lives by the age of eleven.

During the course of working with the Maryam teachings in this book, you will notice yourself changing, sometimes quite rapidly. You may experience new qualities within yourself or a definite enhancement of qualities you were already aware of. Your life is full of signs and symbols awaiting your awareness of them. Events in your life reflect something about you at that moment. The people in your life reflect aspects of yourself. Here, "people" should be understood in the indigenous sense of any being—from humans to animals, to plants, to the ground beneath your feet, to the air you breathe, to the very elements of landscape and climate.

Like metamorphosis, there is a change from one state to another. Your consciousness is expanded so that awareness is expanded. The heart opens further. You are able to give out more love energy as you become more immersed in the cycle of love energy. You are more able to align your personality with the soul to facilitate greater expression of the sacred. This is a process rather than a sudden change.

SEVEN QUALITIES TO DEVELOP

Here are seven qualities that you will develop as you make your way through the Seven Signs. There is no order or hierarchy in these signs of transformation, though you may find that one inevitably follows from another.

A New Awareness

As your consciousness is raised and you make efforts to pay attention to the details of situations and incidents in your life as they happen, you will develop heightened awareness. This is a stress-free awareness in which you detect the energy of love at work in the world—in yourself, in other people, in other beings, situations, and landscapes.

A New Reverence for Life

Heightened awareness of life introduces awe and wonder at the most minute as well as the greatest aspects of Creation. The sacred aspect of Creation becomes a reality and part of your everyday feelings about life as you perceive it. This realization energizes your interaction with All That Is. A new reverence for life can be equally described as love. Love is the force behind creation and love allows us to align with the rhythm of the created universe.

A Sense of Oneness

The world will continually make you aware of your separate individuality, but this is now an awareness in which you can relax because you know—with an inner knowing—that you are part of and an expression of Oneness. You know that you can enter the realm of Oneness by simply finding your heart place and resting in it, as you do in meditation, for example.

An Inner Knowing

Like all the other signs of your transformation, this is a quality of the heart. Whatever your mind or other minds might try to tell you, you *know* the reality of the sacred. It is not a belief or even an act of faith. If you have not already had a confirming experience, you will have one. Inner knowing puts you in touch with your inner healing wisdom, and the spirit of Khokhmah/Sofia becomes a constant companion.

A Glimpse of Fearlessness

An aspect of your inner shaman, your inner warrior, is aroused. You may often recognize a situation where, formerly, you felt afraid. There may have been people who, if they did not actually frighten you, made you feel uneasy. Now you know that there is nothing and no one to fear. You are not separate from others or separate from life. You are part of them and they are part of you. With these warm feelings, you can watch life unfold without expectation or trepidation.

An Agent for Peace and Harmony

You can see that allowing life to unfold is a conscious decision not to offer resistance to the process, not to retreat to the fear-based response, but to offer a love-based response whenever possible. A useful question to answer when faced with a difficult situation or decision is: "What would love do?" It takes courage to be an agent for peace. This is the courage of the spiritual warrior.

A Center of Compassion

With your awareness in your heart energy center, the seventh sign of your transformation is effortless compassion. This is not dependent on morality or the positive tenets of a religion. You are not compassionate because you, or society, think it's a good thing. Compassion is a heart center *energy*, an effortless part of your being. You don't have to think about it. Others will recognize this quality and find themselves gravitating toward you for comfort, companionship, empathy, reassurance, and healing.

With even one of the seven signs of transformation in place, you will find it easier to understand that the universe is supporting you. Your efforts to bring about conscious transformation will further human evolution. We have talked about how it is advisable to avoid the personality's expectation of, and need for, outcome. It may be a glib truism that the journey is more important than the destination, but—along with Maryam—I have addressed you as the spiritual traveler: you have been going somewhere. If you need a sense of destination, it is to be able to consciously allow soul to express the sacred I AM through the person that is you. This happens when you discover who you really are. The discovery takes you back to the circle dance!

TO SUM UP

THE LIVING WISDOM OF THE SIGNS

Healing is certainly about living in the realm of the miraculous, in the realm of greater awareness. With greater awareness you develop a healing consciousness. This is why the ability to heal is a by-product of conscious spiritual development. The Seven Signs point to seven wisdom ways in which Maryam can take you into the realm of the miraculous. Here they are

- Through the wisdom of Sign One, you can recognize the cosmos as what it really is, like finding that water is wine. You can live beyond the opposites as well as live with any of them. As you move toward becoming whole, so your wildness returns.
- Through the wisdom of Sign Two, you discover that there is no barrier in the space-time continuum to distant healing, nor to

your retrieving the original soul consciousness of the child.

- Through the wisdom of Sign Three, you can heal the paralysis induced by identification with the physical alone, healing the paralysis induced by fear.

- Through the wisdom of Sign Four, you discover the balance point of the Seven Signs, and in doing so you lose the fear of want. There is enough of everything and plenty for you to share with others. The heart is an organ of spiritual perception, enabling you to see with the eyes of the soul.

- Through the wisdom of Sign Five, you lose a fear of Nature. You learn how to trust your feelings and learn how to harness your emotions and emotional reactions.

- Through the wisdom of Sign Six, you can heal the inner blindness—a deeper, more serious form of paralysis induced by identification with the physical alone. To be a prophet means to be able to see the whole picture, not just the future.

- Through the wisdom of Sign Seven, you are liberated from the bondage of assuming that your personality—with its body, mind, and emotions—is all that you are. Your true reality is I AM, the same I AM that is in every being and All That Is. Grasping this you are ready to live the heart-centered approach to life.

18

LIVING THE HEART-CENTERED APPROACH

WHAT IS *YOUR* INNER MESSIAH (I AM SOUL) ASKING OF YOU?

Throughout the creation of this book, Maryam has been aware of what I have been sharing with you. In this final chapter—as a twenty-first-century culmination of the wisdom stream sent into the world 2,000 years ago—she updates and enlarges her teachings with an urgent call to practice the heart-centered way of thinking, speaking, and acting. Within the context of each of the Seven Signs, she addresses a personal call to you, the reader, which I render in italics.

Sign One and You

Your sacred task while on planet Earth is to remember and honor your spirituality: to open yourself to allow the expression of your sacred reality and to prepare for reunion with the Source. Through the creation of the individual soul on incarnation, the human is effectively separated from the Source. This process directly affects the unified nature of the emissive and receptive—"masculine" and "feminine"—streams of divine energy. The incoming soul is a divine being, but its separation from the Source also separates the two energy streams. This has allowed human beings to create an energetic imbalance within themselves and within human soci-

eties, leading to destructive human behavior and its negative effects on Nature and the planet. Your sacred task, therefore, is to live life by honoring all that is sacred and creating balance wherever possible.

This considerable task is begun by taking part in the inner "marriage," by reuniting the two energy streams within the context of each person's state of imbalance. How the task may be achieved is described through the story of a common event (marriage) at which something highly unusual takes place. Maryam is hinting that the true significance of the wedding ceremony has been lost. If we were made more conscious of it, perhaps it would positively influence the choice of partner and help us realize the tremendous undertaking to which the wedding commits us. The wedding scene draws attention to the role of ritual and ceremony in maintaining our link with the sacred. This link has become crucial to both individual and world healing because of the suffering caused by our disconnection from the sacred.

Maryam and her followers came from a spiritual tradition that was rich in sacred ritual and ceremony, activities that were conducted daily in home or outdoor gatherings. Sacred ritual and ceremony always address the unique nature of personal imbalance in participants because these activities make contact with the energetic state that each individual presents. This means we should be aware that those leading any sacred ritual or ceremony need to have their masculine and feminine selves well developed and well integrated.

The "marriage" of the two forces will be acted out in different ways according to one's culture. For many of the people involved, marriage is an external activity. But the wedding has to be an internal process if it is to bring personal balance and harmony as well as happiness and fulfillment. How this happens is unique to each individualized soul. Maryam leads us into the necessary internal event through an Aramaic play on words.

Damah can mean "wine," but also "blood," the vital liquid that carries the life force. Water into wine describes the ennobling of the self through sacred ritual and ceremony, culminating in the unification of the two energy streams. There is no timetable about when this will happen. For some it may take a lifetime. The invitation is to recognize how imbalance has manifested in your life. Then look at your community and at the world to see how whole societies have developed along one or the other of the two sacred streams. They will all fail until union can be achieved at an individual and global level. One of the most destructive manifestations of the dominance of one of the energy streams is the tendency to solve all problems with violence and war. The answer is not in what "they" are doing out there. World healing begins with you, and Maryam teaches us never to doubt the power of one person to bring about change. Matter (the body and the world as you perceive it) can be changed—upgraded—through the power of the spirit.

Sign Two and You

Once you have begun the process of bringing your two energy streams into balance, you are ready to embrace your spiritual reality. Having embraced your spiritual reality, express it! No one is born alone. Each incarnating soul receives help and guidance for the journey it faces on Earth. There are no exceptions. No one is beyond loving guidance and assistance, and sacred service does not discriminate. Worldly wealth and power are not barriers to this help and guidance, but how people use or abuse wealth and power will depend on how they adhere to the sacred guidelines given by the soul.

We human beings must address the needs of our "inner child" before the consequences of neglecting these needs emerge as sickness and sick societies. We must also address the needs of the children of the whole world family. Childhood is the stage of humanity most aligned with the soul, and children are the future of humanity. Maryam's question in Sign Two is, Are we raising children to have a consciousness of the sacred?

The evolving sacred being is aware of everything that is happening in its human life. The official's son in Maryam's Teaching Story symbolizes that the masculine energy stream has been severely abused.

Consequently this energy is not as developed as the feminine, hence its crudeness and warring nature. Help in the form of distant healing is always available, but it has to be asked for. The sacred is always present to assist you on your life path. Prayer is a way of harnessing this help from the sacred. You can also take part by practicing distant healing yourself.

Sign Three and You

Paralysis can occur within any aspect of your physical self and your life, but in your heart you know that a healing can occur. The embodied soul will always lead its physical personality self to the healing waters of the feminine energy stream! The relationship between the sacred being and the human person is addressed here. Is the sacred soul directing the life of the human personality or is it the other way around? This question applies to all human beings all of the time.

As Maryam emphasized in the previous Sign, we need to remember that we are never alone and help from the sacred is always available. The challenge may be to walk away from what is safe and familiar.

MORE ABOUT NUMBERS IN THE TEACHING STORY

Maryam points out that the state of paralysis in the story is not solely physical. The thirty-eight years mentioned is a clue to what paralysis represents. We saw how this number was deliberately chosen by the ancient storytellers to represent the time that the Hebrews spent wandering in the wilderness. It was also chosen for its deeper meanings.

The number 3 represents the triangle of human growth and development, and 8 signifies infinity, eternal evolvement, and the number of Maryam. When added together $3 + 8 = 11$, the symbolic number of the enlightened one. In the celebration of sacred union, the two separate energy streams $(1 + 1)$ are joined, making the symbol of union (2).

In the Hebrew *alef-bet,* or alphabet, each letter has a numerical value. Thus 38 is made up of 30 + 8 (*lamed* and *khet*). Lamed means "to learn the knowing of the heart"; khet means "dynamic life and the movement of the body." Thus, the mystical meaning behind the time of paralysis lies in learning that our heart-based inner knowing, rather than the mind alone, allows the soul to direct our lives. Paralysis can occur in any aspect of the formula: 3 + 8 = 11. Maryam describes it occurring in both the Sign One and Sign Two episodes as people fret about what can be done. Sign Three teaches that if we listen, there is an inner knowing that a healing can occur. The embodied soul will always lead its physical personality self to the waters of the great feminine.

Sign Four and You

It cannot be said too often—there is always *enough of everything, and that includes love. In the story of the feeding of the 5,000, it is important to realize why the "miracle" was possible. We are all one, yes, and that is the logical reason for sharing, apart from the spiritual one. The miraculous was possible because Yeshua experienced himself as the I AM Source, therefore the source of anything that is needed. With such a connection to the Source, anything may be manifested on the physical.*

The miraculous is timeless—check out the "miracles" of the Indian avatar Sai Baba (1926–2011), for example. This is one of the great spiritual truths of the heart and why heart-centeredness is essential to develop the new consciousness and the new awareness. The issue of sharing is about the use of resources for the betterment of all. The bread and fishes are significant. Human beings should understand that the Earth and her seas can provide all that each of us needs while undertaking the life journey. The important word here is need, not want. The use of resources for the betterment of all has already become a major issue for the whole of humankind and one that is already leading to the devastation of the resources of land, sea, and air. It has become the root cause of much greed, much poverty, and much conflict.

The answer to the question of how the resources of Earth and Water can be justly shared lies in the story's symbols. The sharing of

Earth resources comes about by living the exhortation in the Torah (as represented by the five loaves, the sources of inner nourishment and understanding) to "love your neighbor as yourself." This is sacred advice. The sharing of Water resources comes about by realizing the soul within both energy streams—two fishes. The counsel of the soul, to be heard within the heart, is that there is always enough. Finally, the message is underlined by the twelve baskets, signifying the senses that serve as a conduit between the soul, physical reality, and the Godsource. Everything *is* the Source and the Source has no limitations, and you can choose to behave as if this is so. The assurance of the sacred is that one person *can* make a difference. The soul is asking you to "feed the multitudes" and not to be overawed by the task in front of you

Sign Five and You
Each and every one of you has to learn the unique nature of your emotional self, how you react to different circumstances, and respond accordingly. This is another formidable task, but the feminine energy stream can assist in this.

You are equipped with everything needed for the soul's life journey on planet Earth. A significant aspect of a human being is the emotional self. There is much confusion around the meanings of words like "feelings," "emotions," and the verb "to feel." Your emotional self is there to help process all aspects of your life and to align your personality self with the pattern of the individual soul self. Your emotional self knows what is right and what is not right for you and tries to align itself with the soul pattern. We have feelings that tell us about this. But invariably the process of alignment is interrupted by the personality self that, in turn, generates its own feelings. This interruption causes the emotional self to be shaped by the life path undertaken and is often in need of healing.

Thus there are two forces acting on the emotional self: the personality with its conditioned mind and the soul. The emotional self reacts to either of the two forces and attempts to process them. You then interpret the reactions of your emotional self as emotions and feelings. The clue to what part is calling to us lies in the heart and the mind. When the soul calls, its language is heard in our heart, rather than our head.

The struggle of the soul to express its divine nature through the personality means that it is crucial for you to develop a thorough understanding and respect for the emotional self. Maryam illustrates this lesson through the dramatic episode of Sign Five, involving fear of water on the one hand and emotional serenity on the other. Water is essential to life and so are emotions, but they both have to be treated with respect.

Sometimes your emotions have to be taken into account when planning the next step on the path of life, and sometimes they have to be put aside and not allowed to interfere with your actions or your progress. Emotions are powerful energies that can be harnessed to promote stronger action or a greater response to a situation. On other occasions it is in your interest to control or rise above these powerful energies. Each one of us has to learn the unique nature of our emotional self and respond accordingly. This task seems daunting, but the feminine energy stream can help.

To trust the spirit within, not to fear that you will fall, may seem like being asked to "walk on water." If this is how you feel, ask for help . . . you will receive it.

Sign Six and You
Open the inner eyes of the soul to see what is happening to yourself, to others, and to your world. Then, your new awareness should be the trigger for right action.

The message here is about the difference between looking and seeing. We humans have developed the ability to be blind to the truth of what is happening to us, to the life around us, and our beautiful planet. In the Sainte Baume cave, Maryam told me that it was only our clouded vision that prevented us from being able to see the truth about life and about our sacred selves. In the Sign Six episode she indicates how we develop clouded vision and then persist in seeing everything through this filter. Clouded vision is represented by a range of characters who express skepticism, skepticism born of logic, cynicism, concern for the letter of religious law, concern for right behavior, form, derision, jealousy, and open hatred. Clouded vision ultimately has its origins in the conditioned mind.

In our twenty-first-century world, Maryam's Teaching Story also points to our physical origins in the mud of the Earth. The destruction of Earth, which is daily taking place, gives rise to tears in the spirit realm. The soul laments the behavior that is bringing internal as well as external destruction. Remember, the figure of Yeshua in the Signs story represents the soul. The spit in the story is the tears of the sacred. Maryam is asking: Does it take the tears of the sacred to make you see? Will you have to destroy everything and be forced to begin again—return to another Earth—before you see? Knowing that you cause your soul to weep should be the trigger for right action. Seeing what you are doing to the planet should be the trigger for right action.

We should return to an Earth-based spirituality and relearn the ways of the Earth. There are still many indigenous groups who continue to offer guidance and help. Begin by listening to the soul voice in your heart and be aware of how you feel in your emotional self when you hear this voice.

There is much talk about healing the planet and the need to heal the planet. However, if healing the planet really means healing the global destruction that continues to be wrought by humans, we should be aware that the planet is quite capable of looking after itself—and its means of looking after itself may not necessarily benefit human beings. We are not separate from any part of the natural world or the rest of the cosmos, so healing the planet is about a threefold strategy. First we need to be aware of what is happening, second we need to work out how to mitigate previous destruction, and third we need to work out how to prevent further destruction.

To prevent further destruction, humans have to reach a certain kind of understanding of the universe. This understanding will demand a new ethical view about human behavior and human needs, rather than wants. A new ethical view about human behavior and human needs will demand a course of action. The necessary course of action will not come about simply by calling the planet "Mother Earth" or "Gaia," but healing consciousness does offer an understanding of the universe based on experience rather than belief.

Healing consciousness, which Maryam's teachings are designed to develop, helps us understand that solutions offered by the thinking mind alone will not solve ecological problems. We need to come from the heart, to be reconnected to the web of life, and this will not happen simply by thinking about it. Only when we are reconnected to the web of sacred life can we can properly address the threefold strategy outlined above.

Sign Seven and You

You have much yet to understand regarding death and resurrection. The last episode in the Gospel of Signs is deliberately told in a form that will provoke questions from my listeners and followers. When considering your life path, the assumption that your journey ends with death is very inaccurate. All life is cyclic. Human life has a beginning and an end, but soul life has no such limitation. You need to be better educated about the death of the physical body, the disintegration of the personality self—including its emotional and mental elements—and the disentanglement and release of the spirit self (soul) from all aspects of physicality.

Most of Maryam's teachings about death and the release of the soul have been lost, but she leaves us with some important guidelines in the episode about Lazarus. Three full days and nights of Earth time are needed for the process of releasing the soul from physicality. Physical death coincides with spirit rebirth. All human beings release their sacred self upon death. This is true resurrection. Lazarus being freed from the burial cloths describes the unbinding of the soul from all aspects of its physicality.

It is the spirit self that can be seen after the physical death experience. Sometimes this spirit self is easily identifiable as its former human counterpart. Great spiritual masters, such as Yeshua, are able to show themselves in their spirit form—as he does after his death by crucifixion where Mary Magdalene was the first to witness the well-known "resurrection" scene. Similarly, a spiritual master may enable a group to see her own or another's spirit "body"—as Yeshua does in the case of Lazarus.

The phenomenon of people being able to see another's spirit body is not a rare or miraculous occurrence. Nurses have recorded how they have seen both the spirit bodies of terminal patients and the spirit bodies of friends or relations who have already "passed over" and have come to help the dying patient. I have witnessed the same phenomena on a number of occasions. Resurrection is the truth that the soul self is released from the body at death. This is what Yeshua means when he tries to explain to his followers that there is no "death."

To put new life into your old body means to at last allow the spirit to express itself in your life, to say goodbye to your old life, to "come out of the tomb."

THE PURPOSE OF SPIRITUAL TEACHING

As Yeshua reiterated many times, from the sacred soul's perspective, a person who is unaware of his own spiritual reality is dead to that reality; if he continues to live like that, he is already dead. The purpose of any spiritual teaching, therefore, is not to found a religion, nor to indoctrinate another into a religion, nor to preach religion. The purpose is to teach people how to facilitate the expression of their sacred soul and how not to stand in the way of that expression. After all we came here to express the Divine through the medium of a personality with its physical body, mind, emotions, *and* its permanent link with the sacred. If a religion has lost sight of this purpose, it has no useful function in the lives of those who practice it or are urged to practice it; such a religion will simply perpetuate separation from the Source, from each other, and from the rest of Creation.

We are talking about consciousness here. Soul expression depends on your conscious alignment with the sacred. Your purpose, then, is to align your personality consciousness—that you identify as "you"—with your soul consciousness. Maryam's Seven Signs explain how to do this. Sign Six tells what happens when you align all levels of consciousness— you can now see with the eyes of the heart. You see yourself, life around you, and the world from the divine perspective. Before the two consciousnesses were aligned, it was as if your soul was in bondage to your personality while at the same time your personality was in bondage to itself. Sign Seven is about this resurrection of inner vision and the resurrection of the soul within your being.

As Maryam teaches in her update to the Seven Signs Story, there are many ways, such as ritual and ceremony, to engage your whole being—body, mind, and emotions—in the purpose of consciousness alignment. Alignment is a form of remembrance, for deep within each of us is recognition and remembrance of who we really are. It is up to you to seek out those practices that help, encourage, and develop your conscious alignment. A clue is that they should resonate with you and give you joy.

HOW YOU WILL MAKE A DIFFERENCE

Your mind may well ask the question: Does putting Maryam's teachings into practice really make any difference to the parlous state of the world? You will recall that at the start of our journey with her Teaching Story, Maryam directed our awareness to the fact that everything in Creation is divine energy. The implication is that everything is sacred—there is nothing that is not sacred. It is worth repeating that energy follows thought. If we change our thinking, and the way we use our minds, we change energy patterns. Because We Are All One, each change in energy affects the whole; therefore, each change in mental activity affects the whole. When enough people like you make the wisdom teachings their own through practice, it will bring about a sea change in human consciousness toward a heart-centered way of life. History tells us that this is the key to ensuring that we, the whole Earth family, and the planet can flourish in balance and harmony.

No matter how difficult the tasks ahead, the story of Yeshua, as told by Maryam, shows you that it is possible to achieve them when soul is invited into your life.

YOUR INVITATION

You are invited to see how your own path aligns with the teachings of the Seven Signs, and to celebrate how you have already found ways to do this. Perhaps you have taken part in workshops such as finding an ecological approach to living, or how to integrate the masculine and feminine energy streams, or understanding death and dying, for example. We have instant access to news from all parts of our "global village." I wonder what your response is to what you see and hear.

I still feel a pain in my heart as I watch the collapse of institutions, the violent attempts to solve a country's problems, the widespread suffering of whole populations, and the toll on the natural world caused by human action. But on a table in front of me is a magazine that tells of a hundred and one opportunities to align with the teachings of the Seven Signs by joining with others in activities that celebrate the sacred soul and its Earth home. This confirms my inner knowing that we are all, in our way, working toward world healing. If you and people all over the world continue to work through the transformation program offered by the teachings of the Seven Signs, the promise of the beach vision can be achieved.

Next to the magazine is a more academic journal with an article about the way women especially are making pilgrimage to the cave of Sainte Baume. In interviews many of these women indicated that they treated their experience as a rite of passage, so their emergence from the cave felt like a rebirth. If you cannot get to the cave, the Seven Signs will take you through a similar process. You could even take this book with you, or call upon her, when visiting a sacred place devoted to Maryam or indeed any aspect of the feminine.

Maryam chose a sequence of teaching stories in which each had a magical, dreamlike quality flowing with timeless wisdom. This is because they each describe the work of the soul. Dreams embody the surreal, and this allows them to show you revelations about yourself and your life that are often out of the reach of your everyday consciousness. The French poet and founder of surrealism, André Breton, once said: "Love is when you meet someone who tells you something new about yourself." Through working with her Teaching Story, may you meet the Mary Magdalene who will lovingly tell you something new about yourself, something new about your life, something new about the world, and perhaps something new about herself.

GLOSSARY

Pronounce *kh* as *ch* in Scottish *loch* or German *ich*. The sound *ah* at the end of Hebrew and Aramaic words is a long ā; sound *e* as in *fete* without making a diphthong; sound *i* as *ee* in *seen;* sound *o* as in *lot,* without making a diphthong, as in *phone;* sound *u* as *oo* in *moon.* Hebrew tends to stress the last syllable, Aramaic the penultimate syllable. An apostrophe (') indicates that syllables should not be run together.

There is no sound or letter *sh* in Greek. This sound becomes *s.* In this language masculine words and names have to end in *s* in order to be declined. See, for example, the derivation of *Jesus* below.

Abbreviations are Aram.= Aramaic; Eng.= English; Gk.= Greek; Hb.= Hebrew; pl= plural; Skt.= Sanskrit.

abba: Aram. father, parent, ancestor, founder.

Alahah: Aram. God, Sacred Unity, Oneness, the Source, the I AM.

Andreas: Gk. Andrew, brave.

angelos: Gk. messenger (hence English angel, see malakh).

anthropos: Gk. human being; as used in the gospels: a complete human being, one who has realized his spiritual reality.

Ar'ah: Aram. Earth, Nature, embodied reality, all individual forms.

221

aura: the subtle energy around someone or something, perceived as light; from Greek *avra;* see kevod.

b: Hb, Aram. in, at.

bet: Hb. house, the second letter of the Hebrew alef-bet; since ancient times a common first half of a village name (e.g., Bet Anyah [Bethany]).

bishah: Aram. evil, unripe, not fit for purpose, not ready, out of rhythm or harmony.

chakra: Skt. wheel, subtle energy center.

Christ: from Gk. khristos, anointed one (see messiah); Greek version of Hb. *mashiakh.*

Coptic: the final phase of the language of ancient Egypt where many heretical Christian groups had settled. Coptic was written in a form of the Greek alphabet.

damah: Aram. blood.

derash: Hb. interpretation.

Earth: I capitalize the name of our planet to emphasize its sacred reality within a sacred cosmos (Hb. *olam*).

Earth family: the beings of the animal, plant, and mineral worlds that share this world with us.

eder: Hb. flock.

El: ancient Hebrew word for God; common as an ending to a name (e.g., Rapha-el).

Eliyahu: Hb. the prophet-shaman Elijah.

Elohim: Hb. Source of powers, a plural form meaning God. This fascinating word indicates that the Source is the source of an infinite number of "powers" or attributes.

ena: Aram. I am; when emphasized as ena'ena: the I AM; occurs in the Fourth Gospel whenever Yeshua is recorded as saying "I am . . ." (mistranslated as referring to himself).

Essene: ancient ascetic sect of Judaism; there is scholarly conjecture that Jesus and John the Baptist might have been trained in this sect; see also Nazarene.

Eyeh-asher-eyeh: Hb. the name of God as given to Moses; literally "I am that I am" as well as "I will be what I will be," indicating a continuing energetic reality rather than a being of some sort. But the humanist rabbi Sherwin Wine remarked: "How can you talk to creative energy?" Reader, what's your take on this one?

Filippos: Gk. Philip.

Galil: Hb. The Galilee; known in Israel as "the Galil."

gnosis: Gk. knowing based on inner experience rather than intellectual knowledge.

Gnostic: signifies the emphasis on transcendental experience of the One (gnosis)—the meaning taught by Yeshua and Maryam—as opposed to mere intellectual understanding or ritual observance. When capitalized in this book: for some, a form of revolutionary Galilean Judaism, later of Christianity, based on the principal of gnosis.

God/Godsource: (see Source, I AM, and YHVH).

Gospel of Signs: the name used in this book that was given by certain academics to the first eleven chapters of the Fourth (John) Gospel.

Goy: Hb. a Gentile (non-Jew), pl. goyim.

I AM: the name of the Source discerned by Moses during a shamanic vision quest (see page xii). In this book the Source is often referred to as, in the words of Yeshua, "the I AM." The I AM Presence is the indwelling sacred, the experience of the Source within. In Jewish mysticism known as the Shekhinah, a feminine aspect of the Source.

Ishoah: Aram. Jesus, also Eshoah (see Yeshua).

Iyov: Hb. Job.

Jesus: English form of Yesous, itself a Greek form of Yeshua and Ishoa, now having a pronunciation that gives no clue to the original Semitic name.

Judea: Latin version of Hb. Yehudea.

Judas: Greek version of Hb. Yehudah, a Jew.

Kayafa: Hb. Ciaphas, High Priest at the time of the Crucifixion.

kefa: Aram. rock, stone.

kevod: Hb. glory, the subtle energy around a person or thing, perceived as light.

Kinneret: Hb. Sea of Galilee (is a lake).

koinonos: Gk. companion, lover; from root concerning communion or intimacy; a term in The Gospel of Philip referring to Mary Magdalene.

kham: Hb. warmth. The letters KhM are an ancient Semitic root signifying womb, a dark place of safety and nourishment. They occur in the Aramaic words for love (rakhmah), bread (lakhmah), and in the name of the Hebrew feminine force Wisdom (khokhmah).

khaye: Aram. life, the life force. In Hebrew occurs as the toast *le khayim,* "to life!" (literally: "to lives")!

Khokhmah: Hb. wisdom, the divine feminine embodiment.

Khristos: Gk. anointed one, hence English Christ, see mashiakh.

lakhmah: Aram. bread. Hb. lekhem.

Lazarus: Greek version of Hb. Eleazar.

Lebah: Aram. heart.

lekhem: Hb. bread.

lev: Hb. heart.

Logos: Gk. the manifestation or expression of all things; word.

magdal: Hb. tower, watchtower.

malakh: Hb. messenger, spirit messenger or conveyer (later as angel).

mare: Aram. lord, master (not in sense of having servants).

Maryam: Aram. Hb. Miriam; Eng. Mary; Gk. Maria.

mashiakh: Hb. anointed one, hence English messiah.

mayah: Aram. water.

meltah: Aram. word, substance, divine energy, story, a complete entity.

messiah: anointed one (Hb. mashiakh; Gk. khristos).

midbar: Hb. wilderness, "that which resonates."

midrash: Hb. interpretation, especially of a sacred text; from root derash.

Mikhah: Hb. the prophet-shaman Micah.

Miriam: Hb. Mary; Aram. Maryam.

Mishlei: Hb. The Book of Proverbs.

Nag Hammadi: village in northern Egypt where a collection of Gnostic, Christian, and other sacred texts were found in 1945; has given its name to the translations known as the Nag Hammadi Library, which have shed new light on Jewish, Christian, and Gnostic groups in the first few centuries CE.

Nak'dimon: Hb. Nicodemus (Greek/Latin translation).

nafshah: Aram. soul-self, soul.

Natan'el: Hb. Nathanael.

Natzaret: Hb. Nazareth.

Nazarene: one of many ascetic sects of ancient Judaism; a title sometimes applied to Jesus, "the Nazarene."

nefesh: Hb. soul.

netivah: Hb. path, way of being.

nuhrah: Aram. light, intelligence, clarity, illumination.

olam: Hb. universe, world, from a root implying concealment: the sacred is concealed within Creation.

ouroboros: Ancient symbol showing a snake or dragon eating its tail. Represents a dynamic cycle, especially something that constantly re-creates itself; a cycle that begins again as soon as it ends. Also represents continuous primordial unity.

Oxyrhynchus papyri: over 500,000 papyrus fragments found by archaeologists at the ancient city of Oxírringkhos (el-Bahnasa) in Upper Egypt, written in a range of ancient languages. The collection—still only partly translated—has already revealed a number of versions of The Gospel of Thomas.

Palaestina: Latin. The Roman province of Palestine.

pardes: Hb. orchard, garden.

Parushim: Hb. Pharisees. As Roman oppression was accelerating, the collapse of biblical Judaism, various Jewish groups struggled to respond to the crisis. The Pharisees tended to side with the poor against the Roman occupation and its Jewish allies, initiating the reforms and new interpretations of Torah that became Rabbinic Judaism. Some scholars believe that Yeshua began his adult life as a member of this group.

peshat: Hb. simple, single, upright, literal.

peshitah: Aram. simple, single, upright, literal; the name of the Aramaic Bible.

Peter: a disciple originally named Shimon (Simon), then nicknamed Kefa (Aram. rock, stone); Gk. Petros, hence Eng. Peter. Could be a nice Aramaic play on words because "kefa" in Greek refers to the head. So his nickname could have meant "Rocky" or "Rockhead," which might have referred as much to his stubbornness or ignorance as his steadfastness.

petros: Gk. rock, stone; Greek form of Aramaic kefa; nickname of Shimon in the Fourth Gospel, hence his English name Peter.

Pilatus: Pilate, Roman governor of Palaestina at the time of the Crucifixion.

pistis: Gk. faith, confidence in someone or something.

qadash: Aram. holy, sacred.

rab: Aram. great, as in rabbi (my great one).

Rabbi: Hb. teacher, great one.

Rabbuni: Aram. "my dear Teacher."

rakhmah: Aram. friend, love.

razah: Aram. mystery, secret, symbol, sign.

remez: Hb. allegorical, poetic.

reshit: Hb. beginning. From root RSh: a force radiating light and warmth outward.

rishah: Aram. beginning.

Rosh Hashanah: Hb. New Year (literally: the beginning of the year).

rukhah: Aram. spirit (pl. rukhot), breath, wind, air.

Semitic: in this book, the cultures, worldviews, and languages of the ancient Middle East and the Levant.

Seven Signs: (capitalized) the seven seemingly miraculous happenings centered on Jesus, as told in the first eleven chapters of the Fourth Gospel.

Shabbat: Hb. the seventh day; Sabbath: from Friday sunset to Saturday sunset. In Judaism the day devoted to prayer and other spiritual activities. In the orthodox religion, there are many laws pertaining to behavior on that day.

shalom: Hb. peace, to be fulfilled or complete, harmony on all levels of being; the name Salome is a Greek form.

shaman: Now a term in general use, originally a word from the Siberian language meaning "holy person," or a person in touch with spiritual reality. The ending -man does not refer to the masculine gender.

Shekhinah: Hb. divine presence seen as a feminine force or energy.

shelamah: Aram. peace, to be fulfilled or complete, harmony on all levels of being.

shemah: Aram. name, light, sound, vibration, atmosphere, vb. hear. Interestingly, also Hb. meaning "listen!"

sherarah: Aram. truth, right, harmonious, that which liberates and opens possibilities.

shivah: Hb. the week of mourning (mentioned in Sign Seven).

Sign: when capitalized, one of the Seven Signs of the Gospel of Signs.

sod: Hb. secret, mystery, hidden.

Sofia: Gk. wisdom (hence English Sophia).

Source: (capitalized) in this book, the all-encompassing creative force, the I AM, All That Is, Life. This book prefers non-gender terms for "God," and a concept of the Source, and the sacred, as simultaneously imma-nent in—and transcending—the whole of the cosmos. The I AM.*

Spinoza: the radical Dutch Jewish philosopher Barukh Spinoza (1632–1677) contended that everything that exists in the universe, includ-ing spirit, is one reality. He regarded "God" and "Nature" as two names for the same reality. The philosophy of Spinoza provides the basis for Humanistic Judaism.

Story: when capitalized in this book: the teachings of Mary Magdalene, as found in the first eleven chapters of the Fourth Gospel, told in the Semitic oral tradition as a number of episodes (including the Seven Signs) as one complete story.

Sukkot: Hb. sheds, booths, temporary structures built with vegetation when the Hebrews were wandering in the wilderness; sing. sukkah. The midautumn festival celebrated five days after Yom Kippur; one of the festivals mentioned in the Fourth Gospel, attended by Jesus and the followers.

tabah: Aram. good, ripe, ready, fit for purpose.

Tanakh: Hb. the Hebrew scriptures (renamed by Christians as the "Old Testament").

tar'ah: Aram. door, gate.

Teaching Story: when capitalized in this book, the teachings of Mary Magdalene as found in the first eleven chapters of the Fourth

---

*Asked by Rabbi Herbert Goldstein whether he believed in God, Albert Einstein said that he believed in "Spinoza's God who reveals himself (itself) in the orderly harmony of what exists, not in a God who concerns himself with the fates and actions of human beings" (see also "YHVH").

Gospel, told in the Semitic oral tradition as a number of episodes (including the Seven Signs) as one complete story.

tikkun ha nefesh: Hb. repairing, or healing, the soul. Personal transformation. At a deep level the phrase means to recognize the physical being as sacred and to behave accordingly. Therefore, to be heart-centered.

tikkun ha olam: Hb. repairing, or healing, the world. It is considered the responsibility of every Jewish person. At a deep level the phrase means to align oneself with the world as sacred. To do this means first engaging in tikkun ha nefesh (personal transformation). In this book, the joint purpose of Maryam's teachings.

Torah: the five books of Moses (the first five books of the Jewish bible). Along with the rest of the Jewish bible, today considered the spiritual basis of Judaism.

urhah: Aram. way, the light that reveals a path or hidden possibility.

Wisdom: Hb. khokhmah, Gk. sofia.

Ya-akov: Hb. Jacob; from whom the Twelve Tribes of Israel are supposedly descended.

Yarden: Hb. flowing. Name of River Jordan.

Yehudah: Hb. Judea; a Jew.

Yekhez'k'el: Hb. Ezekiel.

Yerushalayim: Hb. Jerusalem.

Yeshayahu: Hb. the prophet-shaman Isaiah.

Yeshua: Hb. Jesus, Joshua, meaning "God saves" (pronounced Yeshua); Aram. Eshoa/Ishoa; Gk. Yesous; Latin. Jesu; Eng. Jesus. A masculine name cannot be declined in Greek unless it ends in *s*. Greek does not have the sound *sh*. Thus Yeshua becomes Yesous in Greek. The *y* sound takes on the letter *j* in Latin. This is then pronounced in English as the sound *j* in John, so that Yeshua in English has now become Jesus (pronounced Jee-zus), well distanced from its Semitic origin. The word yeshuah also means "the Holy One (Yah) saves."

YHVH: Hb. The unpronounceable "name" of God, as given the second time to Moses in the book of Exodus (6:2–3).* See also "Source."

Yokhanan: Hb. Aram. John.

Yom Kippur: Hb. The fasting Day of Atonement (*kippur*), considered by many Jews to be the holiest day of the year.

---

*In December 2013, in a foreword to the readings for Exodus, Rabbi Arthur Waskow of the Jewish and multifaith Shalom Peace Center, Philadelphia, suggests an exciting, if controversial, "renaming" of God. Just as it was essential for the Hebrews to rename God after leaving Egypt, we, too, in our turbulent times need to rename and reconceptualize the name "God." YHVH cannot be pronounced in Hebrew because there are no vowels between the consonants. Instead, Rabbi Waskow urges us to know and experience God in our own generation through "pronouncing the Unpronounceable Name by simply breathing—*YHVH* with no vowels, as the Interbreath of Life, the ONE that keeps all life alive, that intertwines, interbreathes, the trees and grasses and ourselves." (The interbreathing spirit of all life is, of course, the I AM, as featured in this book.)

SUGGESTIONS FOR FURTHER READING

These books offer many different points of view about the background, teachings, and lives of Jesus and Mary Magdalene.

Abram, David. *The Spell of the Sensuous*. New York: Vintage Books, 1996.

Adam, Betty Conrad. *The Magdalene Mystique: Living the Spirituality of Mary Today*. Harrisburg, Pa.: Morehouse Publishing, 2006.

Angelo, Jack. *The Distant Healing Handbook*. London: Piatkus Books, 2007.

———. *Distant Healing*. Boulder, Colo.: Sounds True, 2009.

———. *The Self-Healing Handbook*. London: Piatkus Books, 2010.

———. *Self-Healing With Breathwork*. Rochester, Vt.: Inner Traditions, 2012.

Angelo, Jack, and Jan Angelo. *The Spiritual Healing Handbook*. London: Piatkus Books, 2007.

Barrett, Patricia R. *The Sacred Garden: Soil for the Growing Soul*. Harrisburg, Pa.: Morehouse Publishing, 2000.

Bauman, Lynn C., Ward J. Bauman, and Cynthia Bourgeault. *The Luminous Gospels: Thomas, Mary Magdalene, and Philip*. Telephone, Tex.: Praxis Publishing, 2008.

Bauman, Lynn C. "How Exclusive is the Gospel?" *Journal of Contemplative Reflection* 1, no. 3 (1998).

Bernstein, Ellen, ed. *Ecology and the Jewish Spirit: Where Nature and the Sacred Meet*. Woodstock, Vt.: Jewish Lights Publishing, 2000.

Bloom, William. *The Power of the New Spirituality: How to Love a Life of Compassion and Personal Fulfillment.* Wheaton, Ill.: 2012.

Botkin, Daniel B. *No Man's Garden: Thoreau and a New Vision for Civilization and Nature.* Washington, DC: Island Press, 2000.

Bourgeault, Cynthia. *The Meaning of Mary Magdalene: Discovering the Woman at the Heart of Christianity.* Boston, Mass.: Shambhala, 2010.

———. *The Wisdom Jesus: Transforming Heart and Mind—a New Perspective on Christ and His Message.* Boston, Mass.: Shambhala, 2008.

Brown, Raymond E. *The Community of the Beloved Disciple: The Life, Loves, and Hates of an Individual Church in New Testament Times.* New York: Paulist Press, 1979.

Bruteau, Beatrice, ed. *Jesus through Jewish Eyes.* Maryknoll, N.Y.: Orbis Books, 2001.

Buhner, Stephen Harrod. *The Secret Teachings of Plants: The Intelligence of the Heart in the Direct Perception of Nature.* Rochester, Vt.: Bear & Company, 2004.

Castle, Leila, ed. *Earthwalking Sky Dancers: Women's Pilgrimages to Sacred Places.* Berkeley, Calif.: North Atlantic Books, 1997.

Charlesworth, J. H. *The Beloved Disciple: Whose Witness Validates the Gospel of John?* Valley Forge, Pa.: Trinity Press International, 1995.

Chilton, Bruce. *Mary Magdalene: A Biography.* New York: Doubleday/Image, 2005.

Chopra, Deepak. *The Third Jesus.* New York: Harmony Books, 2008; London: Rider, 2009.

Christ, Carol P., and Judith Plaskow, eds. *Womanspirit Rising: A Feminist Reader in Religion.* New York: HarperOne, 1992.

Cooper, Rabbi David A. *God is a Verb: Kabbalah and the Practice of Mystical Judaism.* New York: Riverhead Books, 1997.

Davis, Avram, ed. *Meditation from the Heart of Judaism: Today's Teachers Share Their Practices, Techniques, and Faith.* Woodstock, Vt.: Jewish Lights Publishing, 1999.

De Boer, Esther A. *The Gospel of Mary: Listening to the Beloved Disciple: Beyond a Gnostic and Biblical Mary Magdalene.* New York & London: Continuum International, 2005.

Douglas-Klotz, Neil. *The Hidden Gospel: Decoding the Spiritual Message of the Aramaic Jesus.* Wheaton, Ill.: Quest Books, 1999.

———. *The Genesis Meditations: A Shared Practice of Peace for Christians, Jews, and Muslims.* Wheaton, Ill.: Quest Books, 2003.

Dubisch, Jill, and David Winkelmann. *Pilgrimage and Healing.* Tucson, Ariz.: University of Arizona Press, 2005.

Errico, Rocco A., and George M. Lamsa. *Aramaic Light on the Gospel of John.* Smyrna, Ga.: Noohra Foundation, 2002.

Fedele, Anna. *Looking for Mary Magdalene: Alternative Pilgrimage and Ritual Creativity at Catholic Shrines in France.* New York: Oxford University Press, 2012.

Fortna, Robert. *The Fourth Gospel and Its Predecessor: From Narrative Source to Present Gospel.* London and New York: T&T Clark International, 2004.

Frankel, Ellen. *The Five Books of Miriam: A Woman's Commentary on the Torah.* New York: Putnam, 1996.

Gottlieb, Lynn. *She Who Dwells Within: A Feminist Vision of a Renewed Judaism.* New York: HarperCollins, 1995.

Hareven, Shulamit. *The Vocabulary of Peace: Life, Culture, and Politics in the Middle East.* San Francisco: Mercury House, 1995.

Haskins, Susan. *Mary Magdalen, Myth and Metaphor.* London: HarperCollins, 1993.

Hirsch, Samson Raphael. *The Hirsch Haggadah.* New York: Feldheim, 1988.

Houston, Siobhán. *Invoking Mary Magdalene: Accessing the Wisdom of the Divine Feminine.* Boulder, Colo.: Sounds True, 2006.

Ilan, Tal. *Jewish Women in Greco-Roman Palestine.* Peabody, Mass.: Hendrickson, 1996.

Jewish Publication Society. *The Jewish Study Bible.* New York: Oxford University Press, 1999.

Jones-Hunt, Jackie. *Moses and Jesus: The Shamans.* Ropley, England: O-Books, 2011.

Jusino, Ramon K. "Mary Magdalene: Author of the Fourth Gospel?" *The Beloved Disciple,* 1998. Available at http://ramon_k_jusino.tripod.com/magdalene.html (accessed August 23, 2014).

King, Karen L. *The Gospel of Mary of Magdala: Jesus and the First Woman Apostle.* Santa Rosa, Calif.: Polebridge Press, 2003.

Kumar, Satish. *Earth Pilgrim.* Totnes, England: Green Books, 2009.

Kushner, Lawrence. *Honey from the Rock: An Introduction to Jewish Mysticism.* Woodstock, Vt.: Jewish Lights Publishing, 2000.

Lee, Bernard J. *The Galilean Jewishness of Jesus*. New York: Paulist Press, 1988.

Leloup, Jean-Yves. *The Gospel of Mary Magdalene*. Rochester, Vt.: Inner Traditions, 2002.

———. *The Gospel of Philip: Jesus, Mary Magdalene, and the Gnosis of Sacred Union*. Rochester, Vt.: Inner Traditions, 2004.

———. *The Sacred Embrace of Jesus and Mary: The Sexual Mystery at the Heart of the Christian Tradition*. Rochester, Vt.: Inner Traditions, 2006.

Malachi, Tau. *St. Mary Magdalene: The Gnostic Tradition of the Holy Bride*. Woodbury, Minn.: Llewellyn Publications, 2006.

Marsh, John. *The Gospel of Saint John*. London, New York: Penguin, 1991.

Meyer, Marvin, ed. *The Nag Hammadi Scriptures*. New York: HarperCollins, 2007.

Meyer, Marvin. *The Gospels of Mary: The Secret Tradition of Mary Magdalene, the Companion of Jesus*. New York: HarperSanFrancisco, 2004.

MacDermot, Violet. *The Fall of Sophia*. Great Barrington, Mass.: Lindisfarne Books, 2001.

Maclean, Dorothy. *To Honor the Earth*. New York: HarperSanFrancisco, 1991.

Moore, Thomas. *The Soul's Religion*. New York: HarperCollins, 2002; London: Bantam Books, 2003.

Pearce, Joseph Chilton. *The Death of Religion and the Rebirth of Spirit: A Return to the Intelligence of the Heart*. Rochester, Vt.: Park Street Press, 2007.

Rasha. *Oneness*. Charlottesville, Va.: Hampton Roads, 2008. Also published as *The Divine Wisdom of Oneness*. Mumbai, India: Jaico Publishing, 2008.

Robinson, James, ed. *The Nag Hammadi Library*. New York: HarperSanFrancisco, 1990.

Roth, Andrew Gabriel. *Ruach Qadim: Aramaic Origins of the New Testament*. Mosta, Malta: Tushiyah Press, 2005.

Schaberg, Jane. *Resurrection of Mary Magdalene: Legends, Apocrypha, and the Christian Testament*. New York & London: Continuum, 2002.

Shapiro, Rabbi Rami M. *Proverbs: The Wisdom of Solomon*. New York: Bell Tower, 2001.

Soesman, Albert. *Our Twelve Senses: How Healthy Senses Refresh the Soul*. Stroud, England: Hawthorn Press, 2006.

Skolimowski, Henryk. *Let There Be Light: The Mysterious Journey of Cosmic Creativity*. New Delhi, India: Wisdom Tree, 2010.

Spong, John Shelby. *Liberating the Gospels: Reading the Bible with Jewish Eyes*. New York: Harper SanFrancisco, 1997.

Starbird, Margaret. *The Woman with the Alabaster Jar: Mary Magdalen and the Holy Grail*. Santa Fe, N.Mex.: Bear & Company, 1993.

———. *Mary Magdalene, Bride in Exile*. Rochester, Vt.: Inner Traditions, 2005.

Stein, David E.S. ed. *The Contemporary Torah: A Gender-Sensitive Adaptation of the JPS Translation*. Philadelphia, Pa.: Jewish Publication Society, 2006.

Tedlock, Barbara. *The Woman in the Shaman's Body: Reclaiming the Feminine in Religion and Medicine*. New York: Bantam, 2005.

The Holy Bible, New Revised Standard Version. Oxford and New York: Oxford University Press, 1995.

Van Lohuizen, Wali. *A Psycho-Spiritual View on the Message of Jesus in the Gospels: Presence and Transformation in Some Logia as a Sign of Mysticism*. New York and Oxford: Peter Lang Publishing, 2011.

Vaughan-Lee, Llewellyn. *The Return of the Feminine and the World Soul*. Point Reyes, Calif.: The Golden Sufi Center, 2009.

Waskow, Rabbi Arthur, and Rabbi Phyllis Berman. *Freedom Journeys: The Tale of Exodus and Wilderness Across Millennia*. Woodstock, Vt.: Jewish Lights Publishing, 2012.

Winkler, Gershon. *Magic of the Ordinary: Recovering the Shamanic in Judaism*. Berkeley, Calif.: North Atlantic Books, 2003.

INDEX